# PLANTS IN TUBS,
# POTS, BOXES AND BASKETS

# PLANTS IN TUBS, POTS, BOXES AND BASKETS

With 21 colour plates and 35 other illustrations

## LESLIE JOHNS

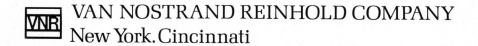
VAN NOSTRAND REINHOLD COMPANY
New York. Cincinnati

Van Nostrand Reinhold Company Regional Offices:
New York  Cincinnati  Chicago  Millbrae  Dallas

Copyright © 1974 by *Leslie Johns*
Library of Congress Catalog Card Number 74-7865
ISBN 0-442-24143-7

Printed in Great Britain
Published in 1974 by Van Nostrand Reinhold Company
A Division of Litton Educational Publishing, Inc.
450 West 33rd Street, New York, N.Y. 10001

1  3  5  7  9  11  13  15  16  14  12  10  8  6  4  2

# CONTENTS

# LIST OF ILLUSTRATIONS

Photographs not acknowledged are taken by the author

# INTRODUCTION

So that we understand one another right from the beginning it will be helpful to define the idea of gardening in tubs, pots, boxes and baskets and then to set some limitations on our definition. To me this means growing plants of all types, from annuals and aquatics to trees and shrubs, in containers of all types, large and small, portable and static, with and without drainage facilities but in each case entirely separated from the soil, the original mother earth. The limitation I would set would be to keep these contained plants out of the home. I would also keep them out of the greenhouse.

But although house plants and tender greenhouse subjects will be excluded, our homes are too important and offer too many advantages to be ignored completely. We will be growing plants on balconies and roof tops; we will be using window boxes and hanging baskets as containers. We will even be making brief incursions from patio or terrace into the garden room, into porches and doorways. We will, in fact, be exercising our wits and flexing our fingers in a good many ways to make the most of the plants we grow.

And when you really come to look at it, just count the benefits, advantages, blessings and beauties offered by container gardening. You don't have to have a garden in the first place but can grow your plants quite well on a roof, on a balcony or even in a window box perched high above a city pavement. No heavy digging is involved, which opens the hobby to the very young and the very old, the hale and the weak, the crippled and even to many who are confined to wheelchair or to bed. There is no dreary weeding involved, or so little as to make it almost a pleasure! Under certain circumstances even the weather loses its vital importance, for containers can be planted up in the dry of shed or garage, can be protected from the worst of winter frosts and winds, can be placed in sun or shade, even in warmth to hasten early growth.

Container-grown plants can be moved from place to place according to the effect you wish to achieve. They can be used to make a hedge or barrier, to indicate a pathway, to protect another plant or block a doorway, to hide or disguise an eyesore, to furnish and civilise a bare and bleak yard. Being separate, containers can enclose different, tailor-made soils, so you can have a rhododendron growing happily in its acid soil in one container while beside it, equally contented, grows *Syringa microphylla*, its roots lime-fed. You can have large containers and small containers, tall or shallow, plain or decorated, painted or natural, antique or modern, in almost any material it is possible to imagine and in a series of designs which are constantly being widened in scope and improved.

The opportunities offered by container gardening, then, are almost limitless, the only real restriction being imposed by size. Surprisingly large trees and shrubs can be grown in surprisingly small containers so long as the soil or other compost is rich and sustaining and the roots are always kept moist, but to grow a really large tree or shrub to maturity is not normally possible. Theoretically there is no reason why it should not be done if the container itself is large enough, but a huge container defeats its own purposes and intention.

As might be expected, large plants in small containers tend to become somewhat dwarfed and to grow more slowly than they would if planted in the open ground. But this is not a bad thing. Just as a house plant fed and watered too well tends to outgrow the home space allocated to it and to be an embarrassment rather than an embellishment, so most (though not all) plants growing in containers are more convenient and more suitable if they are kept within limits and not allowed to romp away as they might if their roots were unconfined. Yet as all contained plants are in effect pot plants, they can always be moved on to a larger container should the need arise.

We are beginning, then, to see one or two differences between gardening in the garden soil and gardening in a container. There is, in fact, a considerable difference in technique and while I intend to discuss and explain the results of my own experiences in growing plants in containers in the country and in the city, at ground level and on the roof, I must admit that some of the subtleties of this specialised form of gardening can only be learnt by experience.

It's a pleasant way of learning!

L.J.

# 1

# SPECIAL CARE

Any plant growing in a garden bed or border must compete with its neighbours for food, moisture, air, light, space, and above all for the attention of the gardener, who will clear away the weeds from its feet, water and feed it when necessary, prop and secure it against strong winds and generally aid it in its struggle for life.

But a container-grown plant is not only free from competition, it commands the individual attention of the gardener, receives food and water designed specifically for its requirements, suffers no weeds, grows in tailor-made compost. So what does such a plant do? It gives of its best.

Yet one of the reasons for the general high level of quality of container-grown plants is that they command individual attention. Whereas garden plants are treated collectively, those in a tub or trough are looked at singly. We speak of the 'rose bed' and the 'heather border', but of 'the sedum in the sink trough'. One of the many plants in a bed or border may exist for days weakened by disease or subjected to insect attack, and it is not until the casual glance is caught by some change in colour, some warping of the leaves, that it receives its necessary attention, its diagnosis and finally its cure. It is

insignificant mainly because it is one of a crowd, and as one of a crowd it grows in the same soil as its neighbours, receives the same amount of food and moisture, is warmed by the same sun and buffeted by the same winds.

Our container-grown plant, even if it is one of several growing in the same tub, has its roots in a special soil, has had its location chosen with care so that it receives just the right amount of sun, shade and protection, is examined carefully to see if it shows signs of drought or sickness and has competition ruthlessly torn away if it shows signs of being overcrowded.

No wonder then that container-grown plants so frequently look so well, and no wonder also that container gardeners so frequently look so happy.

But as with all honest currency there is another side to the coin. Our container-grown plant has so many advantages that it is no wonder it grows well. And who gives it these advantages? The gardener. So the gardener mixes special soil for the plant, the gardener moves it from sun to shade or in the lee of a wall, the gardener examines it daily, waters it, feeds it, sprays it, removes competitive plants if it seems overcrowded. The gardener, then, is a busy man, or more frequently a busy woman, for women generally not only have greater opportunity for container gardening than men but they have a much greater talent. They are cleaner, neater, pay greater attention to detail, have a better eye for beauty, are more versatile, inventive, imaginative. Women are also more patient and more thorough.

All these virtues are helpful to the man in the garden; they are essential to the woman with her containers. The most important thing to understand with all container gardening is that detail is important, nothing can be left to chance, constant attention must be the rule.

Only the experienced container gardener will understand how rapidly the condition of plants can change. One trough can be so well watered in the morning that puddles form on the paving beneath it from the excess moisture from the drainage holes. Yet that same plant can be limp with dehydration in the afternoon. Or it can be shining with health in the morning and covered with sooty aphids by evening. The process of growing plants in containers is a highly artificial one and it succeeds only when the various necessities of attention are provided at the right time.

This does not mean that container gardening is a time-consuming business or even that it is particularly demanding in attention. The various necessary activities can be carried out in a few minutes and without great expenditure of energy, but the important thing is that they are carried out promptly.

When a plant has been growing in garden soil for some time it has learnt to some extent to adapt itself to conditions prevailing. It may send out strong and woody roots to anchor itself securely in a position where the winds tend to rock it. The finer and hair-like roots will travel through the soil in search of

food and moisture in the form of a solution of salts or chemicals. If the weather is dry these roots will dig deeper, travel further in search of the moisture that the plant so badly needs. The other plants in the immediate vicinity will help protect our specimen plant by shielding it from the stronger blasts of the wind, by shading it from the constant blaze of the sun, by taking their communal share of the frosts and the snows.

Even the largest of our plants, our huge and noble trees, have a relatively enormous area in which their roots can roam to collect the food and moisture necessary for life. Equally, some of the plants we grow in our containers have a considerable cubic space in which their roots can travel, but on the other hand some have so little root room that they can exist only when food and water are applied to the roots so frequently as to approximate to hydroponic treatment (the growing of plants in liquid solutions). Where space is so limited the sheer quantity of soil or compost around the roots must also be limited, hence it will dry out quickly. Because it requires frequent watering the foods in the soil quickly become leached out and must be replaced. The soil itself, overworked and exhausted, thins quickly, becomes lifeless, and must consequently receive refreshing mulches of active, energetic, humus-rich soils to restore its vitality.

All plant roots require not only food and moisture but also air, without which the plant will die just as surely as if it received no water. This is one reason why careful attention to the drainage of all containers is vital. Although it is possible for the skilled gardener to grow indoor plants of many kinds in containers without drainage holes (but with special provision for drainage nevertheless), I believe this to be impossible out of doors. A container without adequate drainage will quickly fill with water in a summer shower or even a winter drizzle and the plant it holds will begin to drown.

The provision of drainage holes in the base of a container means that when water is applied at the top, whether naturally or artificially, this courses through the soil and when this has absorbed all it can take the remainder trickles out again through these holes. In doing this it carries out two vital functions. First as it courses through the soil, gravity-fed, towards the drainage holes in the base, it sucks down after it air from the atmosphere. Secondly, because the excess water does not lie in the base of the container, stagnant and unhealthy, root rot leading to the eventual death of the plant is prevented.

This aeration of the soil is so important and so little appreciated that it might be well to illustrate it in another way. If a sponge is held under water the air it holds will float upwards in the form of bubbles and the space it occupied will be taken up with the water. Now if the sponge is lifted out of the water again the water it holds will begin to trickle out from the base and air will gradually fill the vacated spaces at the top and move downwards as the water trickles out. You will be left with a sponge which contains both water and air. This is exactly how we wish our soil to be.

The speed with which the soil in a container dries out will obviously depend to a great extent on weather. But it will also depend on the material from which the container is made, a porous stone or terracotta container drying out more quickly than when the soil is held in plastic, lead, fibreglass and similar impervious materials.

Many containers, particularly the many excellent types made from the various forms of plastic and fibreglass that are now being produced, come to us

Cacti and succulents of many kinds will grow well together in all kinds of containers including glazed vessels like this willow pattern bowl. No drainage holes are necessary but the potting compost should be open in texture and placed above a layer of drainage materials

13

without drainage holes. This is for the understandable and laudable reason that they may thus be used either indoors or out. When they are used out of doors, drainage holes should be made in them and some have special 'weak' spots which can easily be punched out. But it is worth stopping to think for a minute before doing this.

Knowledge of local weather conditions can help us with our container gardening in one minor but important respect. We can tailor the drainage of our containers according to the type of climate we may expect. For example, if we can expect heavy or persistent rain over a considerable period we will allow for plenty of drainage material in the base of the containers and larger-than-normal drainage holes, also set in the base of the containers. But if the weather will be hot and dry and we know that one of our major tasks will be to keep the roots of our plants moist in their sun-baked pots, then our drainage should not be so sharp and the drainage holes we make should not be in the base of the container but in the sides, just an inch or more up from the base, depending on the depth of the container. This will allow for a certain reservoir of moisture to be held by the pot, and although it will not guarantee a moist soil at all times it will mean that watering need not be carried out quite so frequently, and also that should this service be forgotten or omitted for some reason the plants will have access to sufficient water to keep them going.

I have stressed the importance of providing good drainage in our containers mainly because this is the best method of allowing healthy air to get to the plant roots. So when a container is watered and we watch the water coursing through the soil and finally issuing again from the drainage holes we will know that simultaneously the roots are receiving health-giving air. But there will be occasions perhaps when this moisture, running, trickling, seeping or dripping from the base of the container, may very well be falling onto the balcony of the apartment below or even spoiling the clothes of passers-by in the street. There will be occasions, then, when it is well either to water with greater discretion than is normal or to provide some kind of a drip tray or other facility for preventing the total escape of water. This can be important, too, where the plants in the containers are receiving a liquid feed. It is all very well allowing water to run to waste, but when this water contains a solution of not inexpensive chemicals designed to help the plants to grow it seems a great pity to let it run to waste. A drip tray or other means of catching the excess moisture will allow this to be used again.

For several reasons it is wise to lift all containers off the floor or ground just sufficiently to allow air to circulate underneath. This aids and simplifies drainage. It discourages the congregation of insect pests. It tends to discourage the rotting and warping of certain materials and to prevent over-active roots finding the drainage holes and burrowing down through them to the soil or paving beneath.

If containers are raised like this it is possible to slip a drainage tray under them while they are being watered. Two or three similar trays, perhaps of differing sizes, can be a worthwhile investment, being shifted about from container to container as the watering proceeds, the contents being returned once again to a bucket or some other collecting point.

When window boxes are being installed, and under certain circumstances containers used on a balcony, drip trays should always be provided. Just as

Handsome modern concrete containers can be stacked to give varying heights if required ▷

14

measures must be taken to ensure that a window box is completely safe and secure and cannot fall into the street below regardless of the intensity of the wind or the energy of the window cleaner, so steps should always be taken to see that no water can drip onto the street below or even onto the face of the building. This is a matter of common courtesy as well as caution.

It is well to think of matters like this before installing a window box or any other kind of container for plants. An empty container may be light in weight but one which is filled with moist soil can be quite impossible to move or lift. So always fix window boxes securely in place before filling them with soil, and if you intend that certain other containers shall be moved about from place to place on the terrace or patio or even to different positions in the back yard, make provision for this before filling the containers and so anchoring them permanently.

Occasionally the ground is sufficiently level and smooth to allow wheels to roll over it, and here the built-in rollers which some containers possess are very useful, although as a general rule it will be found more satisfactory to have instead a small platform mounted on easy-roll wheels. Where two people cannot lift a container onto this platform for rolling to another situation, either because of its weight or its awkward shape, it is usually possible to make use of a lifting device something like a stretcher. Two stout poles are used and these are lashed securely to the sides of the container so that they are parallel and can be used by two people (or more if necessary) to lift the container onto the platform or even to carry it to its new location.

Container-grown plants are a part of the design of the area. They should be considered, like all garden plants, from the point of view of colour, shape and

16

P.17

*Facing page*
*(above left)* Modern materials are inexpensive, easy to handle and durable. These plastic containers are filled with a light, soil-less potting compost, ideal for window boxes and ledges

*(above right)* A gay assortment of pansies, fuchsias, geraniums and forget-me-nots in tubs, baskets and boxes

*(below left)* Waist-level containers mean easy maintenance, especially useful to older people who have difficulty in bending

*(below right)* Pansies in plastic saucers, lifted off the ground on a short tripod. Good for winter and spring display, pansies in containers should be moved into the shade in summer

texture. But we are faced not only with the plants but also with their containers. If a container is filled, for example, with spring-flowering bulbs then these will make a gay splash of colour at the appropriate season, but for the remainder of the year the container will present a somewhat uninteresting appearance unless the bulbs are removed and replaced by some other kind of plant.

The container itself should be of sufficient architectural interest to play a worthy part in the overall design even when it either contains no plants or while the plants are so immature as to be comparatively insignificant. Site your containers carefully. Merely because there is an empty space in the yard, by a doorway or on the terrace this is not sufficient reason for placing a container of flowers there. In fact it may very well be quite the wrong reason, for space is as important in garden design as in any other form of visual art and it is often the case that greater visual impact can be achieved by allowing plenty of vacant space in one area and then grouping a collection of containers and their plants together nearby.

Container gardeners tend to collect containers at random. If they see a pleasant shape they buy it and a genuine antique is a constant challenge. Having exactly the same tendency I would be the last to discourage it, but I do urge that greater control be exercised over grouping and siting. Do not mix container shapes, colours or textures, but instead separate them and group together stone or terracotta or plastics, regardless of what plants they may contain. If you have several bowls all filled with, say, pansies, this is not enough to create a unity. They will look all wrong if they are growing in containers of differing materials or colours, although difference in shape does not always have the same importance.

Remember that containers can be sited in three

P.18

*Facing page*
*(above left)* Contained plants will fit into the smallest space. Where no true garden exists a variety of plants grown this way offer a pleasant and easily cared for substitute

*(above right)* Terrace pots and patio containers are a delightful decorative means of linking the house with the garden

*(below left)* Cascading plants in window boxes give full value since they cover such a large area. Feed regularly and remove faded flowers to ensure lengthy blooming

*(below right)* This attractive porch shows plants in several types of containers. Note that wooden types lose water more quickly and in hot weather will need watering two or three times a day

B

Bulbous plants are ideal for container gardening. Although these tulips are spring-flowering, there are also summer-, autumn- and winter-flowering kinds which can be used. Non-bulbous plants such as these myosotis, set among the tulips, will provide attractive contrast and help mask the bulbs as they fade

planes, not just two, and that the third, or vertical plane, is usually the least crowded. Lift some of your containers off the ground. Even a matter of a few inches will create added interest and where it is possible to raise a pot several feet to bring it more or less to eye level you will be giving it much greater dramatic value. The best way of doing this is to use the classical pillar or column, but there are several other possibilities according to the amount of imagination you bring to the subject.

Bear in mind always when raising a container from floor height that it is extremely heavy. Make sure that it is safe. A raised container can so easily be unbalanced by a casual move, by a playing child, even by an excited dog, and when upset it can cause injury to people as well as damage to furniture or to the container itself. Always make doubly sure that the container is absolutely safe and solid and that no accidental jolting or shaking can dislodge it from its elevated position.

# 2

# THE ROOT OF THE MATTER

Plants in the conventional garden have their roots in mother earth, the provider of all. And because natural soil is just that, the provider of all, it must be a sort of lowest common denominator, something that will suit all plants of all kinds and grow them not too badly, not too well. Most gardeners spend a great deal of time and sometimes a comparatively important sum of money to make their soil more effective. Yet their efforts are like opening an umbrella to keep a thunderstorm off a garden. It has taken millions of years for the soil on this planet to reach its present condition and it will take millions more before we see any significant change in it.

But in his container the gardener can place a soil mixture which has been specially made to his requirements. He can, in fact, have a dozen different containers each holding a different soil created to a recipe aimed at producing a specific effect on some specific plant or family of plants. What opportunities this presents to us!

But container gardening has its roots very much in the soil of the conventional garden and it will be helpful to have a quick look at this.

A way of examining a handful of soil would be to drop it into a glass of water and stir it vigorously.

After a time it would begin to settle and clear and we would see on the base of the glass the odd stone or two. Above this would be a layer of sand, becoming finer as it reached upwards, and still clearing in the water and dropping a fine blanket over the materials in the base of the glass would be clay. On top of the water would be floating the odd tiny stick, leaf or other piece of vegetation.

The aim of every gardener is to get his soil into the condition of the middle layers, neither stony nor composed of clay.

The material that is floating on top of the water adds body and goodness to the stony or sandy soils and helps also to break up the heavy and solid structure of the clay. The material is organic waste, decaying leaves and other vegetable matter, dead insects and animal droppings. This is the material that gives a soil life, and in general terms it is well to have a really thick layer visible on top of your water. The reason why it is so valuable, apart from the fact that it improves the actual structure of the soil, is that it encourages bacterial activity. Plenty of this material in the soil means that billions of bacteria will be working away invisibly, drawing out of the soil the various salts and minerals necessary to plant growth and making them up into solutions acceptable by the roots. This material, so valuable both to the conventional and to the container gardener, is generally known as humus and is readily available.

One source of humus that is also rich in plant food is special garden-made compost. It may not be possible for some container gardeners to make this themselves because they have not the space or the facilities, but any gardener with a tiny plot should be able to provide himself with considerable amounts of this helpful material. If every bit of waste vegetable material is saved and put towards the making of compost it is surprising how much can be collected. This waste material includes such things as lawn mowings, hedge trimmings, fallen leaves, the outer leaves of cabbage and lettuce, all kitchen vegetable waste, even such materials as egg-shells and tea-leaves. To these are added soil and perhaps some farmyard manure, if this is obtainable, and proprietary agents which accelerate decomposition to produce rich and enormously helpful humus.

There are several different ways of producing this compost, though they are basically much the same in principle. Start off with a flat piece of land in a more or less hidden part of the garden. Build on this a little platform of woody material such as tree branches, under which air can circulate. Then on top of this place a layer of vegetable material about 4in thick and cover this with a 2in layer of soil. If you use lawn mowings, do not make the layers so thick that they exclude air, and if you use hedge trimmings or prunings, make sure that they are chopped or smashed so they are soft enough to rot down quickly. Keep the heap neat and tidy and build up layers of this kind until a convenient height is reached. Ideally the heap should be boxed in on all sides (but not on top) so that it heats up well to kill any weed seeds or

fungus that may be present. Water it just enough to keep it moist but not wet. Every layer or so add a little accelerating material, and when watering use liquid fertiliser to bring extra richness to the heap. Liming will help reduce excess acidity too. If the mass is large it may need turning after a few weeks, the outside to the centre and the top to the bottom. But from three months or so onwards you should be seeing a fine, dark, granular substance quite different from the original materials from which it was made. Always keep a compost heap going.

There is a tendency for home-made composts of this kind to be somewhat acid, so a sprinkling with lime while it is being made will bring it to a more neutral state. There is nothing wrong with an acid soil and some of our most beautiful plants, such as rhododendrons, insist on it, but it is important to see that the soil does not become TOO acidic as few plants will flourish under such conditions. There are a number of soil-testing kits available from garden stores which are inexpensive and easy to use. Generally the principle is that a little soil is shaken with a liquid that is provided and the colour of the solution is compared against a chart to determine whether the soil is acid or alkaline, and sometimes even whether certain minerals are absent.

Most soils are more or less neutral and will grow any kind of plant with a greater or lesser degree of success. But for those plants which insist on a certain type of soil, gardening in containers holds a special bonus as it is a relatively simple matter to use an acid soil in one container for a lime hater and an alkaline soil in another container for a lime lover.

The measurement of acidity and alkalinity in soil and in water is by a pH scale, a complex mathematical relationship of the concentration of hydrogen ions in the soil. Neutral on this scale is 7.0. Acid soils and waters have a lower number and alkaline a higher number. Although the average is 7.0, on the whole a slightly acid soil of about pH 6.5 is regarded as the best for most plants in the garden, but, once again, as we are gardening in containers we can use whatever soil we like although a certain discretion is necessary. Because rhododendrons must have an acid soil it does not mean that the more acid the soil is the better they like it. No soil should normally be allowed to go below about pH 5.0 or 5.5 or above about pH 8.0.

It is quite easy to raise a pH figure, that is to reduce the acidity or increase the alkalinity of a soil, merely by adding a controlled amount of lime. But to increase the acidity is considerably more difficult in open ground because of environmental pressures. An alkaline soil, for example, is probably lying above limestone and any amount of treatment to make it acid will succeed only in a limited way for a limited period. But a soil in a container is isolated from its surroundings and so it can be treated with acid peat or an acid compost to lower the pH figure to an acceptable level.

If he has a garden of his own the container gardener is sitting pretty. He can use his own soil in his containers, treated with peat or with sand, with compost and with fertilisers so that it is exactly as he wants it for his various purposes. But if he has no garden where does he obtain his soil? He can, of course, rely on friends or relatives who do own a garden. On the other hand he can buy his soil just as he might buy his bulbs or his trees.

There are a considerable number of 'manufacturers' of soil who make up a standard product to some agreed recipe and market it in conveniently sized bags through garden stores and sometimes even through chain stores. To satisfy the greatest number of users these soils are usually more or less neutral and it is sometimes possible to buy separate additives to change the pH, and separate fertilisers to give the soil a more concentrated richness. Many of these soils, perhaps most of them, have a brand name which identifies them and at the same time gives some kind of guarantee of their quality and their consistency, an important matter if we are buying several bags of what we believe to be a uniform product. Prices are not high, although obviously they are higher than the cost of home-produced soils.

One of the benefits of most of these packaged and branded soils is that they have been sterilised. You know that they will not contain insects, diseases or viable weed seeds. This is a great help, for apart from anything else weed seeds alone can cause much trouble and distress. Some will remain viable for a remarkably long time and the mere disturbance of the soil will be enough to encourage them to germinate. This being the case it is wise, where possible and convenient, to sterilise any soil that you take from the garden to use in a container as a seed compost. If, however, you are merely planting a young tree or shrub in your container then it is not really worth while. Small electric soil sterilisers can be bought quite cheaply. They consist essentially of a metal box with closely fitting lid and a heating element sealed away in the base. Soil is placed in the box and the heating switched on. After a few hours of this heating the soil will have reached a heat where insect and disease have been killed and any weed seeds rendered sterile. To save time and increase the certainty of success it is wise to cover the steriliser with a heavy blanket or some other similar material to keep the heat in the box rather than allow it to be dissipated in the air.

A small quantity of soil can be sterilised even without this equipment by tying it up in a large piece of material. The bundle so made is suspended in an ordinary domestic steamer and allowed to 'cook' for an hour or two. This again should kill off all organisms and seeds.

But, as I have said, sterilised soil is really helpful only when seed is to be sown in it and our main requirements need be less sophisticated and expensive. Many nurseries and plant centres sell soil mixtures of various types, some as branded products and some of their own mixing. You can buy, for example, a large bag of good rich leafmould, a bag of garden loam and a bag of coarse sand. Mixed in various proportions this will fill a number of containers at very little cost.

Remember too that you can effect considerable savings by an intelligent appraisal of plant needs. For example, you may wish to grow some bright and colourful annuals in a large and deep container. There is no reason why the whole of the body of this container should be filled with your special soil. Instead you can fill the base with stone, rubble or whatever you like so long as you allow not less than 6in or so of soil for the plant roots. Remember, however, that if you do this the drainage is likely to be very sharp and the little plants will require frequent watering. In a case like this it is helpful to use a soil mixture which is particularly spongy and water retentive. This is easily achieved by adding a fair proportion of peat to the soil mixture.

On the other hand many planting mixtures are available today which contain no soil at all, being generally made up from various grades, mixtures and kinds of peat. Some of these no-soil mixtures, as they are sometimes called, are specially designed for growing seeds and some for plants, and there are also certain brands which have been so mixed that they are suitable for seed sowing, for immature plants,

24

Many perennial plants grow well in containers. If these are to be permanent tenants, it is a good plan to plant bulbs deep down in the container where they can remain after their tops have died down. Such plantings need dissembling every three or four years when the bulbs and plants can be divided and planted anew

and for shrubs and trees—a mixture in fact that will do for any plants of any type.

These no-soil composts have so many advantages that for container work they are largely replacing soil. First of all they are very light in weight, a matter of the greatest importance to the average small container gardener. They are clean, odourless and sterile, easy and pleasant to handle. They cannot be overwatered, by which I mean that the peat has so open a texture that water rushes through quickly and out through the drainage holes. Yet as might be expected these peat mixtures absorb and hold water well.

One difficulty that does arise with some (though not all) of the peat-based no-soil composts is when they have been allowed to become too dry. They can then be very difficult to water again unless considerable patience is used. Water merely rolls off the surface, trickles down the side of the container and out through the drainage holes in the base. The only way to combat this is to be patient and water by degrees, preferably damping the soil surface with a fine spray first to make it absorbent again. If the container is comparatively small or if it consists only of a traditional flowerpot, then there is a temptation to plunge this completely into a bucket of water. It is unwise to do this unless you can exercise complete control over the operation, for the tendency is for the entire root ball of peat to leave the pot and float to the top of the water, disintegrating gradually.

These no-soil composts have received wide acceptance by commercial growers and so that the peaty material can be used direct from the sack it has in most cases been treated with balanced fertilisers and trace elements to make it suitable as a growing compost for the greatest possible number of plant types without any further attention. This is a help, of course, and producers generally suggest that plants growing in these composts will require no further feeding for a period of up to about two months or so. Make sure about points like this before you use any new compost you have bought. While it is probable that no real harm would be done to your plants by giving them this double dose of fertiliser, it is equally certain that you would do entirely unnecessary damage to your pocket!

An alternative to constant feeding is frequent mulching. Plants growing in containers gradually use up their soil and it is quite noticeable that the level gradually falls over a long period. This provides space at the top of the container for the addition of fresh soil or a layer of no-soil compost. An inch or two of fresh material like this is a real tonic to the plant or plants in the container, and where soil levels have not fallen sufficiently it is sometimes a helpful plan to scrape away a little of the top soil, very carefully so as not to damage any surface roots, and then to add a mulch of fresh soil.

# 3

# TYPES OF CONTAINER

Among the vast number of types and shapes of plant containers that are available to us, the most attractive are those that have some affinity in their basic material with the soil. Stone containers and those made of various types of clay seem to have an inherent suitability about them, a sense of fitness, a hint of relationship. But the genuine antiques among them are today almost impossible to find and then at a price which makes them more suitable for the safe deposit vault than the balcony or terrace.

Our choice of containers depends, not on the flowers, but on the surroundings, the environment in which they are to be placed. A graceful stone urn filled with a tumbling mass of nasturtiums would look right at the end of the drive leading to the flight of steps before the gracious nineteenth-century Surrey or Vermont family home and it would look entirely wrong trying to hide the trash or garbage can in a London back yard. The squalor would be emphasised, pinpointed, by introducing the alien note whereas it would tend to be disguised if the slovenly yard contained an old bucket brimming with fiery nasturtiums. The same flowers, different surroundings, and entirely different atmospheres.

These are two extremes, of course, and most of us are concerned less with stately homes and squalid back yards than with our average home set in pleasant but semi-urban surroundings, or perhaps in a city block. The containers we can most easily obtain and most happily afford are generally of plastic, usually in designs and of colours which although by no means offensive set one wondering uneasily whether it is quite the right material to use for such a purpose. Yet if fitness for the job were to be considered rather than aesthetics, plastics would win hands-down every time.

Most of us suffer from a phobia about plastics resulting from the time (almost within the living memory of many of us) when plastic substances were first introduced and in order to gain acceptance were disguised to look like the real thing. Hence plastics became synonymous with substitutes, with cheap imitations, and seem to have retained this label ever since. This is a pity, for most plastic containers available today frankly admit their constitution and may in fact even boast of it as a particular virtue or quality. Some manufacturers still produce plastic trying to look like wood or stone but as this becomes increasingly unnecessary they become increasingly fewer.

Plastic is ideal for plant containers because it is light in weight, colourfast, practically everlasting, inexpensive, clean and easily cleaned, available in a vast number of shapes, sizes and designs, watertight at all times yet easily pierced for drainage holes, capable of being painted, strong and not subject to cracking or splitting in rain, sun or heavy frost. These are qualities that should endear the material to us, for they can be attributed to only a few of the other materials used for the manufacture of gardening containers.

One recent type of plastic container which has appeared on the market has still another virtue—it is made of reconstituted waste materials. So something useful and inexpensive has been created out of something that has been thrown away and would have tended to pollute the atmosphere if burnt, and the environment if left lying about. This should be a great encouragement to us. The containers that have been made out of this newly created waste material are largely experimental in shape, unusual and progressive, but any shape could be reproduced perfectly well.

As plastic can be painted, a container can not only be given a particular solid colour to blend with its surroundings or the plants it is to hold, but it can have any kind of pretty or crazy design or pattern put over it. It would be possible, for example, to paint your house name or number on the container by your front door.

Fibreglass, basically different from plastic and yet having many similar qualities, has most of the virtues of plastic and some additional ones of its own, the chief of which is its ability to copy so closely the appearance of some other materials, notably metals, as to be almost indistinguishable from them until touched. Fibreglass is particularly good at matching

Genuine antique containers are today difficult to find and expensive to buy. But, like this urn, so great is their charm, that even damaged and restored specimens are worth collecting

Containers always look best when bursting with bloom. This simple moulded asbestos saucer would be far less effective with fewer pansies in it

lead. So few genuine lead containers of any kind exist today that only the most inaccessible or the most untransportable dare be placed on show, and yet there exist many exquisite reproductions in fibreglass, quite the same in every possible way until they are actually touched and found to be warm rather than cold to the fingers. Prices are high, which may be one reason why this material has not spread its wings and adopted a style and a personality of its own. Slightly more fragile than most plastic materials, fibreglass will shatter, split or chip if subjected to considerable strain, but otherwise it would seem to be as light, as colourfast, etc—and as such, as useful.

For certain simple shapes in plant containers there is a material composed, I believe, of asbestos sheeting, moulded, shaped or pressed into bowls, dishes, saucers and other uncomplicated designs of pleasing proportions. Comparatively heavy and as against plastics possibly somewhat brittle, containers made of this material are good to look at and almost always fit happily into their surroundings because they have the facility of growing old while still young. By this I mean that they quickly and comfortably dress themselves in a becoming grey-green mossy stain so suited as a foil and background for vivid flowers. This material is particularly recommended as a container for mesembryanthemum plants, their intense and startling colours held and cushioned, a 4ft diameter of crocheted colour against the black of the no-soil compost and the dignified grey-green of the container. Although small containers are available, perhaps the most successful of the asbestos designs are comparatively large, the material appearing to be most comfortable when making wide curves rather than tight corners, probably because the designs appear to be shaped out of large sheets under pressure. They are not expensive and invariably look better planted up than they do naked and awaiting purchase.

Quite different, considerably more expensive but wholly delightful are some of the designs which have appeared in comparatively recent years in artificial stone. I say some of the designs advisedly, for a few are somewhat bizarre although the majority are exquisite and approximate to the classic patterns of the past. They are very heavy and should be regarded as permanent ornaments rather than as portable containers. Some are also somewhat soft and crumbly and need careful handling. Because they are heavy some of the larger designs are difficult to move into position and edges and corners are apt to be broken or rubbed off. However, this very softness is a good quality in that it encourages the stone to age quickly and take on an appearance of antiquity. This artificial stone also appears to harden and toughen as it matures, although once it has been placed in position it is difficult to judge this point. More and more of these artificial stone products are appearing on the market and as techniques of manufacture improve it is possible that prices will drop.

Clay, pottery and terracotta designs are also to be seen more and more often, some of them excellent reproductions of classic designs, and some modern and unusual. This material is particularly fitting for plant containers, being pleasant in appearance and colour, solid and weighty, slightly water-absorbent, weathering well, reasonably strong if treated with care, and obtainable glazed, semi-glazed and unglazed, plain and patterned in the widest possible variety of shapes and sizes. There is probably a greater eastern influence on pottery than on containers of other materials, for clays of various types were used and baked many thousands of years ago and in fact plant containers have been found which date back to the great days of the Egyptians. And today the traveller returns from a vacation trip to the Mediterranean area with both mental pictures and photographs of many plants, exotic and familiar, growing in the widest variety of pottery containers. It is unfortunate that they are too large, too weighty and too fragile for us to bring home ourselves, but at least we know that their influence is resulting in a wider choice being made available in other parts of the world.

Wood is a material which I like personally but do not find very practical for outdoor plant containers. My own experience is that no matter how carefully timber is preserved, coated, painted or treated, it has a short life compared with denser materials and does not look its best for very long after it has first been installed. Neither does timber lend itself to many attractive shapes or designs,

Traditional clay pots still compare well with plastic, expanded polystyrene and coopered oak at the end of this terrace

although it has an advantage in that it can be tailored to fit a certain space. The well-known coopered tub can look very splendid when it is new but again it does not last long. Iron hoops quickly rust regardless of rust inhibitors and paints, and copper bands seem to last little longer. Certainly if timber is used (and it always will be because of its adaptability and low cost) it should be very thoroughly treated with some form of preservative before it is planted up.

If paint is to be used on timber make sure that it is applied thoroughly, using several coats. The best chemical means of preserving timber is copper naphthenate in solution. This is generally available in most countries in proprietary form under various names and is usually green or brown in colour although there is also a clear form. It should be painted or sprayed onto the timber in several coats and will make it immune to attack from fungi and insects. Unlike creosote it does not have any toxicity towards plants and can be used quite safely. Some kinds of copper naphthenate can be used as a base which can then accept a wax or synthetic polish.

The best timber containers are those made from special woods such as teak, oak, elm or—less satisfactorily—cedarwood. Some of these, beautifully made and most attractive to look at, have received special treatment against weathering, including several final coats of a special lacquer.

Concrete containers, as distinct from imitation or reconstituted stone, are perhaps a little too heavy, too large and too solid for the average garden although they can be absolutely first class for parks and public places. They will last for ever, are completely vandal proof and they are surprisingly neutral and inoffensive when allowed plenty of space and well planted up so that they are full of colour. Simple designs such as flattened cones and shallow saucers

Grouped together because of their terracotta affinity, these containers include a chimney, a strawberry pot, succulent pan, miniature Spanish barbecue stove and an antique urn

seem to be the best for this purpose.

Of the genuine antiques, stone, cast iron, terracotta and lead provide perhaps the greatest value and the greatest beauty. It is still possible to pick up the occasional bargain in one or other of these materials but most are to be seen beautifully gracing the exterior of some stately home or other. Those seen for sale are frequently damaged in some way but the clever handyman can frequently get a bargain by buying one of these and effecting a discreet repair. Or sometimes it is possible to buy, say, pieces of a marble staircase or plinth which can be carefully taken apart

33

and re-assembled to make a distinctive plant container.

Do not neglect the antique shops and the junk stalls for accessories as well as containers. One can sometimes find decorative ironwork for a stand or support, perhaps even for a wall-bracket to contain a number of pots which will disguise a stark wall. Broken cast-iron garden furniture, pieces of ancient farming implements or equipment, old dairy churns, cracked or chipped butter churns, these and many other similar products can sometimes give a charming and unusual atmosphere to the right kind of garden or yard. Remember that chipped or damaged equipment does not matter so much in the garden as it does indoors, and remember too that if a container is cracked so that it leaks, this may save you having to drill drainage holes! Bear in mind the fact that large containers can so often bear in their bellies a smaller, less attractive, more utilitarian container which will do the actual job of holding the soil and growing the plant and so leave the more precious antique merely as an adornment.

On a less grand scale there is still a great deal that can be picked up and adapted for the garden. The thing to have is an imagination that can picture some unexpected object as the container for a particular spot or some particular flowers. Old tin baths, feeding-troughs, hay-racks, hollowed-out tree trunks, a broken sink unit, a chipped stone or marble mortar without its pestle, all these and many more can effectively be pressed into use.

Today it is almost impossible for most of us to afford the rare examples of fine old stone sinks which make such attractive miniature or alpine gardens. And yet perfectly acceptable replicas can be made, with some trouble but little cost, and from a distance these can be differentiated only with some difficulty

P.35

*Facing page*
*Top row (left)* A newly planted strawberry pot. Contrasting shapes and textures of plants give interest. If using conifers, choose only the dwarf and slow growing kinds

*(centre)* Old and new containers in harmony. The brown kitchen jar is filled with a deep layer of drainage material. The trough is plastic and self-watering

*(right)* Pocket containers made with special little areas for individual plants can be used either to hold all one kind of plant or a mixture

*Middle row (left)* Stone containers merge attractively with their surroundings and plants thrive in the cool, porous root conditions

*(centre)* There is really no limit to the diversity of containers which can be used. This attractive plant stand began life as a display unit in a shoe shop. Free-flowering ivy leaved pelargoniums as here are ideal cascading plants

*(right)* Wooden containers should first be made rot-proof. Never use creosote for the fumes will kill. A special copper-based preservative is best

*Bottom row (left)* A beautiful example of bonsai. Dwarfed trees need not only be hand high and some specimens will live for many years in large containers such as this

*(centre)* Sempervivums and many other garden succulents do as well in containers as they do on rock gardens or walls. They need very little maintenance once planted

*(right)* Attractive little alpine strawberries grown here are best in partial shade. Tubs like this need treating with a wood preservative before use

from the originals. The basis is an old, white, glazed sink unit, the kind that itself is going out of use today yet which can still be picked up either for nothing or for a very small sum from builders engaged on restoration jobs. The idea is to coat this sink with a special mixture which dries to look like stone and adheres securely to the white glaze, hiding it completely.

Old, glazed kitchen sinks are heavy, so take your sample to the place where it is to live, prop it on its brick or other supports and treat it there rather than have to transport it after it is finished. The mixture with which it is coated is made up of sand, cement and peat, in the proportions by bulk of 1:1:2 respectively. These proportions can be varied according to the result you wish to obtain. For example, if you cut down a little on the peat and increase the sand you get a finish more like sandstone, and if you increase instead the cement content you get something more like a limestone. These materials are mixed together and water is added to make a thick and heavy mixture which will hold together and not drip when lifted. But it will be found that nothing will make it stick effectively for long unless the sink first receives on its glazed outer surface some sort of a bonding agent. There are a number of inexpensive, quick-acting and highly effective bonding agents which are frequently used for sticking tiles to floors, for repairing various plastic materials and for many general adhesive jobs. Use one of these (it might be as well to carry out a pilot-test first) at a somewhat higher concentration than recommended, on the outside of the sink. Do not bother with the base but cover the sides thoroughly and take the bond over the edges into the interior, but only down to a point where it will be covered with soil or compost.

Before the bonding agent has had time to dry com-

P.36

*Facing page*
*(above left)* How to turn a balcony into a garden. Troughs should follow the lines of the area. From these, plants can climb, rise and cascade. Water up to three times a day in hot climates

*(above right)* Few gardens could be more colourful than these balconies of flats at Macon, France. The main plants used are sun-loving petunias and pelargoniums

*(below left)* Contained plants as a means of extending the garden area. Iron brackets built into the wall hold these baskets. Remember that suspended containers filled with newly-watered soil can be very heavy

*(below right)* A variety of containers, including decorative hanging baskets, make an attractive approach way

C

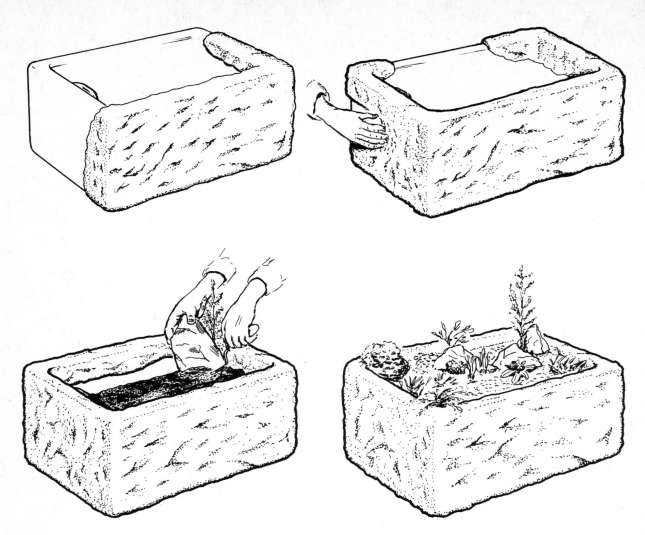

(*Above left*) After painting the glazed sink with an adhesive, the sand, cement and peat mixture will adhere to the tacky surface; (*above right*) patting and pressing the mixture into place leaves a rough and stone-like surface texture; (*below left*) the interior can be left in its original state to be hidden by the soil, rocks and plants as they go into position; (*below right*) the sink or trough is indistinguishable from genuine stone when planting is completed

pletely begin slapping on your peat mixture. There is no way to do this effectively except by hand, using rubber gloves if you care for your skin. Press it on and pat it into place as you go, making sure that the whole of the surface is covered well, no gaps left, and that the peat-cement mixture is at least a quarter-inch thick. Press it securely into place with your fingers and you will find that as they leave their mark in the soft surface these impressions will begin to look like the marks of a chisel on the stone.

When you have finished leave the sink to dry out thoroughly before you attempt to fill it with soil and plant it up. The drainage hole will have been left and the sink will have been so positioned as to have a very slight slope towards this. Plant up in the normal manner.

The incorporation of peat into this special coating mixture has two purposes. In the first place it renders the coating slightly porous so that it absorbs moisture, something that the normal glazed sink could never do. At the same time it gives a slightly softer appearance to the cement mixture, bringing it closer in line with stone. Given reasonable care and protection against knocks from such heavy weapons as lawn mowers, the coating on a sink like this will last for many years, even through heavy frosts.

It is possible to make a complete 'stone' sink of more or less the same materials without using the base of the glazed sink, but it cannot be guaranteed to escape damage from a heavy frost. Prolonged freezing will result in the peat granules bursting and so there may be some flaking when the thaw finally arrives. However, costs are so low that it is sometimes worth taking this minor risk in order to get what can be a most attractive garden ornament.

Exactly the same kind of sand, cement and peat mixture is used, although it is better to make this

Unusual container formed from an old well head ornamented with wrought iron work. Filled with mixed pelargoniums and variegated ivy

39

very slightly more fluid. Two large cardboard boxes, fairly heavy and rigid, can be used as the mould, one larger than the other so that if the smaller stands inside the larger there will be about a 3in gap between the walls all the way around.

The first thing to do is to make the drainage hole. Stand the smaller box inside the larger in the right position and cut a neat hole of the right size through the floor of both boxes. A plastic bottle such as the type used for dishwashing liquids makes a good pattern for the hole and it can be left in position to keep the hole open when the cement mixture is poured in to form the floor.

Take out the smaller box, leaving the plastic bottle or whatever else is used in place. Pour in the cement mixture until it is about 3in deep and tamp or ram this to make sure that it fills the corners and contains no air bubbles. While this is still wet take the smaller box and fit it in position, sliding it over the 'plug' bottle and resting it on the newly laid floor. Then pour the mixture around the sides, again making sure that it fills all the corners and contains no air bubbles. Then leave everything in position while it dries.

The 'stone sink' produced by this method will be strong enough for its purpose if it is not too large. To strengthen base and sides and to make a considerably stronger and more lasting sink reinforce the structure. Ordinary small-mesh chicken wire will do for this purpose. Cut a piece which is roughly the width of the larger box and the same length plus the heights of the two ends. Then cut two more pieces for the sides, the same width as the depth of the box but some six inches or so longer than its length. In the first piece, which is to strengthen the floor, cut the netting to coincide with the drainage hole.

Begin as previously and pour in the cement mixture for the floor, but when roughly half-thick enough place the wire netting in position. The floor piece will bend at each end to make the end walls, but ignore these for the moment and complete pouring the floor, making even more certain this time that the mixture fills all the gaps, that it contains no air holes, and that it covers completely the wire netting, which should be embedded in the centre thickness.

Now place the smaller box in position. The wire netting will be projecting upwards in the two end positions, so take the two side pieces and bend their ends so that they fit into place with a double thickness on the corners. Pour in the mixture around the sides, again making quite sure that the wire netting is well embedded and that there are no air holes. Leave the whole thing to dry and cure.

You will probably find that the cardboard boxes have absorbed so much of the moisture from the mixture that they have become soft. This is an advantage, for they can then be torn away from the sides when the cement has set. If the surfaces look too smooth and artificial they can quite easily be scraped and roughened with a screwdriver or some similar tool. Corners should be rounded and all edges smoothed when the cement has set but before it has completely hardened and cured. Allow at least a week for curing, preferably two, before filling and planting the new sink or trough.

40

# 4

# PORCHES AND DOORWAYS

An attractive entrance to a house is a solace and comfort to the residents and a cheerful welcome to visitors. Nothing can make an entrance more attractive than flowering plants, particularly if they are scented.

The doorway, porch or entrance must be allowed to fulfil its function properly and any decoration it receives must be secondary to this. So whether climbers cover the porch, hanging baskets decorate the entrance, tubs flank the door or other plants climb the walls and frame the entrance, always make sure first that they have been planted a safe distance away and that they are pruned or otherwise disciplined to allow easy and pleasant access. If the entrance space is narrow or if the porch is so small as to allow only one person to stand in it, then keep your plants to the sides rather than permit your pleasure in them to discomfort or embarrass the visitor.

The planting scheme will obviously depend on the type and size of the entrance, but even before this is reached opportunities exist to create an atmosphere of cheerful welcome. Even if there is no pathway up to the house there is nearly always space for a small tub, pot or jar to be placed flanking the entrance doorway, and under circumstances as severe as those under present discussion it would probably be wise to use dignity and discretion rather than a more informal and florid approach, so it is suggested that these tubs contain a narrowly conical conifer or an elegant clipped bay, both of which form a graceful decoration without occupying undue space. An amusing and flippant alternative to this dignified but perhaps rather sombre approach would be to grow in gaily painted tubs on each side of the doorway a tall and ridiculous sunflower.

Neither of these alternatives will take up much space, nor will a hanging basket on each side of the door. It may even be possible to arrange for two or even three hanging baskets, one above the other, to flank the doorway making curtains of colour to escort the visitor on his entrance to the house.

It is unwise to grow plants above a doorway unless this is covered or enclosed as with a porch. The reason for this is simply that in wet weather drips from the foliage are certain to discommode the person waiting in the doorway. Where climbers grow beside the entrance they should if possible be taken along the wall away from the door, although the amount of harm that they may do will depend to a

Beyond the entrance gate to an Italian town house, groups of plants flank a pathway giving the impression of a leafy garden within. Most of them are the hardier types of house plants, safe to use this way in a warm climate. In colder countries they should be used only where the passage way is under cover, but in good light

great extent on the type of plant, its closeness to the wall and its tendency to send out trailing growths which will drip and get in the way.

Whatever is used to decorate a simple doorway, the effect can be heightened if the scheme is given unity by having containers identical and matching the door itself or the flanking wall.

In general it would seem to be wise to use what areas of garden soil are available for the planting of such spreading and colourful material as roses, clematis, jasmine, forsythia and other climbers or shrubs which can be trained to the house wall. Where paving has been laid right up to the house walls on either side of the main entrance then container-grown plants can still be used to give plenty of local colour, but unless really large tubs or troughs can be installed it is perhaps unwise to try to grow large and spreading shrubs such as those mentioned above. They may grow well and they may occupy their positions quite happily for several years, but they will never do as well as the same plants growing in the garden soil and they will never be satisfactory for such long periods.

Use the flanking containers instead for dwarfer but equally colourful plants. Bulb flowers are of course ideal for containers and the range is much wider than is generally grown. The well-known daffodils, tulips, hyacinths can be supplemented by many other attractive bulbs which can be brought into flower not only for spring but for other parts of the year. But while waiting for the tulips or daffodils to grow and produce their flowers we need not be faced with a row of naked containers. Intersperse them with other containers holding plants already in flower.

House walls can give a remarkable amount of protection to plants, protection from wind as well as from cold, and coupled with the slight degree of extra warmth always enjoyed by contained plants this

Whilst humans prefer the shade of this town patio, the attractively contained plants enjoy the reflected light from walls and paving

means that you can probably grow plants here which might be too tender to be grown in the open garden. Experiment, in a small way at first, to see just what possibilities are open to you. Travelling about in various countries, one is frequently brought up with a jerk to see growing (and so often beside a doorway) a fine specimen of a plant that is normally found only in places many miles to the south. This is usually because the house owner has experimented, often with the idea of astonishing the neighbours, and because of envious comment has paid just that little more attention to the container and its plants than they might otherwise receive.

It is when there is a definite porch to the entrance that the real opportunities present themselves. For this serves as a base for exterior decoration as well as an enclosed and protected area capable of more exotic furnishing. Even a tiny porch gives greater opportunity for plants to grow than a mere exposed doorway.

To justify the title, the least a porch can be is a roofed space in front of a doorway. It need not have sides, although there will have to be some means of supporting the roof. Other porch structures may include side walls, sometimes timber, sometimes stone or brick, sometimes dark but usually windowed to some degree. The greatest luxury of all for the plant-lover is to have a porch which is large, well lighted and possessed not only of walls but a door, so that it is in effect a small enclosed outer hallway for the house.

Because the porch has a roof it then becomes possible to grow climbers over it without risk to the visitor at the door, and this is a considerable step forward decoratively. Even if the porch is very small the compulsive decorator will still be able to do some-thing to beautify it without crowding the doorway to a dangerous extent. And other opportunities also present themselves. It may be possible, for example, to insert a hook under the roof at the side and support a hanging basket by this means. It may be possible to train a closely clinging climber around one or more of the support posts, even a variegated ivy would help here to soften and personalise the entrance. And any container used would benefit to a modest extent by the minor added protection it would receive.

Although to suggest heating any but the most lavish and completely enclosed porch would be a reckless and profligate advocacy, there is no doubt that many a porch could be made warmer, more weatherproof and sometimes even bigger without great expense in time and labour. Large sheets of clear plastic sheeting can be erected on comparatively modest frameworks and in certain circumstances and climates it may be an idea to arrange this protection on a temporary basis so that it can be removed again when the worst of the winter weather has passed. A windbreaking hedge or a conifer or two can deflect or soften cold breezes, or on the other hand the pruning or removal of an over-large tree might result in a flood of warm and unaccustomed sunshine into the porch area.

Inside the larger porch decorative opportunities depend on both space and light available. If there are both then almost anything can be done. Bulbs and flowering plants galore, troughs and hanging baskets, bonsai and bottle gardens, a real bower of plant life is possible, capable of being changed according to season and the decorative appearance of the plants so that there need never be any lack of interest but always a welcome and a talking point for the casual visitor.

# 5

# USING WALL SPACE

If one were able to take the wall (or walls) of a balcony and lay it down so that it became a continuation of the floor, it would then be seen just how significant and valuable is this area of gardening space, so often either ignored or used as an after-thought. A wall can vastly increase the gardening area available and nowhere is this more apparent than where space is naturally limited, as on a balcony or roof and even on a patio or terrace. Plants can be grown at the foot of the wall, against the wall to climb up and present the world with a mass of colour in the smallest of horizontal spaces, or even on or sup-ported by the wall by means of holders, hanging brackets, suspended boxes and hanging baskets. So wherever a wall can be used for plants in any way try always to take advantage of it, for with today's land values you will be getting a real bargain!

In the open garden we tend to look on walls mainly as valuable for providing shelter as well as support. It is true that we can grow roses or Virginia creepers up a wall, but more important is the fact that if we live in a cold climate and can rejoice in a splendid south-facing wall we may be able to grow against it *Clianthus puniceus*, otherwise known as parrot's bill or lobster claw because of the shape and colour of the

flowers, or perhaps the white-flowered *Leptospermum pubescens* or the red-flowered *L. scoparium*. The protective and reflective value of a south- or west-facing wall can be very important to us. Apart from the fact that it holds and supports plants at an angle where they will benefit most from the heat of the sun, the wall itself absorbs this heat and gives it off again to the plants growing on it. In the open garden, then, a good wall is much appreciated.

Think how much more valuable it is, therefore, in a place where the total area of the 'garden' is so small that two or three paces in any direction will cover it. A balcony wall, any walls available on a roof space, the wall or walls enclosing a back yard or a patio, these can double the gardening size of these areas, if used to the full, with very little expense in time, money or labour. So important are the extra oppor-tunities offered to us by this vertical space that it may be worth while to stop just for a moment and consider each of these specialist areas in turn to see how best the walls can be used.

A balcony must have at least one wall. It is prob-able that it has two other separations, not perhaps walls in the strict meaning of that word but some kind of physical vertical barrier. Now the house wall

Sun-loving pelargoniums are among our most colourful, useful
and accommodating window box plants

itself, through which one walks to get out onto the balcony, is probably of little real value for gardening purposes as it contains the doorway and almost certainly one window and probably two.

There is also the perimeter of the balcony floor space to consider. Pots, tubs, troughs, urns and the like can be placed all around this space which would otherwise be wasted. On the two sides it may very well be possible to install tiers of flowers, or shelving which will carry rows of pots or long troughs, to present a complete wall of colour to the inside of the room.

Unless window boxes or troughs have been purpose-built and are to a certain extent integral with the structure of the building itself, it is frequently forbidden for apartment or flat dwellers to install their own. This is invariably for the sake of safety, for if an unbalanced and unsecured window box should fall to the street below there could be a terrible accident. It is generally the insurers of these buildings rather than the owners who make such rigid stipulations. On the other hand it is possible to secure a window box, even a series of them, on the inside of a balcony wall or rail, facing into the balcony space; this is actually a more satisfactory position, for the gardener can then himself enjoy the benefit of his work.

Opportunities exist in plenty for decorating a balcony with flowers and plants, but there are dangers too. One of these is the wind, which actually seems to grow in power and intensity the higher you climb above street level. This wind is also less predictable, for it has to whistle through gaps between buildings, around corners and over roof tops so that it is sometimes concentrated or funnelled into a particularly fierce blast. Some form of protection must be given to those areas of the balcony which are particularly vulnerable to wind, and at the same time the style of gardening, the type of plants chosen, must be adapted to the difficulties of the situation.

Exactly the same problems exist for the roof-top gardener except perhaps that he may have more space than the person confined to a balcony. Wind is a real problem on the roof although its effects can be minimised as indicated in Chapter 7. So far as wall space is concerned, this can sometimes be extensive on the roof if the area is surrounded by a perimeter wall; sometimes it is non-existent, just a flat and bleak invitation to the wind, or there may be a compromise in the form of a low parapet or perhaps a mere safety rail. Where no wall exists at all the dedicated gardener can still get his fingers into the soil but he will have to use all his ingenuity, a great deal of patience and possibly some of his spare cash to get interesting results. These matters are again considered in later pages of this book.

Wall space for the window box gardener is at a premium, for the area immediately above the box is almost always occupied by glass, and apart from the problems of growing plants on this unpromising surface, the glass is there in the first place, of course, to admit light to inner rooms and we are seldom prepared to forgo this. But why should plants always be expected to grow upwards? Many of them grow downwards or sprawl quite naturally and these are, in fact, just the plants that we should try to grow here, for they reveal themselves to the inside of the room without blocking too much light and at the same time they hide and disguise the stark and uninteresting sides of the boxes or containers to passers-by in the street and show instead tumbling trails of flower colour. It is surprising just how great an area of flower trail can be produced by a single and comparatively small window box, and so long as the box is secure and the trails are kept under some kind of control then nothing but beauty and pleasure can come from this kind of gardening.

Sometimes a particular window looks out onto a blank wall or a view so unpleasant or depressing that it is better hidden. There is opportunity here to use the whole of the window space for decorative purposes. There will be a diminution in light entering the room but on the other hand what light there is will be filtered through growing green or glowing flower colour, usually an extremely attractive effect. By fixing canes or training-string from the window box to the top of the window space it would be possible here to grow a climber as gorgeous as a morning glory or as plebeian as a decorative and variegated runner bean, which I actually saw myself gracing the home of a town-dwelling friend some years ago.

But valuable though wall space is on roof or balcony it cannot be exploited to the same extent as at ground level. When we are on the ground we normally have a greater area of wall which we can employ in our gardening than under the more artificial circumstances of roof-top and balcony gardening. There is also the matter of sheer convenience, for while it is difficult, dangerous or perhaps even impossible to get at a wall when one is already high in the clouds, it is a much simpler matter on the ground to use steps or a ladder to control a wayward shoot or fix supports in position.

As we have said, there are several ways in which the gardener can use his walls. The most obvious way is to grow plants up them, supporting and training them where necessary to cover a certain desired space. Or the wall can be used as the support for one or more containers, fastened by means of brackets to the main fabric of the building. Although they must exist in

48

On a protected patio it is possible to grow plants in containers that in colder months must be brought indoors. Whitened walls reflect additional light

other parts of the world because of their simplicity, nowhere except in Italy have I seen the plain metal circles jutting out from a wall on a short spike which so efficiently carry a flower pot. An extension of any or all of these ideas is the use of the wall as a support for a structure such as a pergola or skeleton roof which extends from the house or wall and on which plants can be trained, on which they can grow and from which they can be suspended.

All climbers can be grown in containers placed at the foot of a wall and all will make the necessary journey up the wall if given a little initial assistance. The larger the container the more lasting the plants. But it must be admitted that this is not really a very satisfactory way of covering anything but a small wall area, owing to the growth limits which will be imposed by the container size. Nevertheless there are occasions when this way with climbers is necessary, mainly when it is impossible to plant at the base of a wall because the ground area is covered with paving of some kind, or because buried in the ground is service wiring or ducting, or because the foundations of the wall project too far to allow planting.

My own view is that if climbers cannot be grown in the natural soil under a wall it is best not to rely on them for wall covering but to use some other means. My own preference would be for a series of wall-mounted troughs, placed in various convenient and attractive positions on the wall, some bearing gay flowering plants, some carrying a shrub or two to help cover wall space and some carrying small-scale climbers and trailers. By this means the wall could be used to great effect and yet each and every one of the containers could be removed and replaced when necessary or could even be switched around if the growing plants seemed to indicate that this would give a better effect. Simultaneously wall brackets

would allow for the graceful festoons of hanging baskets and hanging pots so that the whole area would be used effectively.

It has already been said that the soil in containers tends to dry out very quickly in warm and sunny weather, and where a number of containers are mounted high on a wall or where there are several hanging baskets requiring water twice a day the plants are apt to suffer unless special arrangements can be made for easy watering. The best thing to do here is to strap the last 6ft or so of the garden hose to a stout bamboo or other light but strong cane so that it is possible to lift the hose and direct its flow directly into the container which may be 15ft or so high on the wall. For hanging baskets it is sometimes a good idea to mount them on the wall via a rope and pulley so that the basket itself (sometimes heavy) can be lowered safely for watering or for the grooming that makes such a difference to their appearance.

When training plants to the wall we have a somewhat greater choice of methods and materials, depending on the size and ultimate extent of the growth of the plant or plants and on the weight or strength of this growth. But whatever the method and material, it will be found helpful to have the support system erected and in position before it is needed. It is often almost impossible to install supports behind a plant which is already growing. If the wire mesh, the trellis, the training-wires or whatever, seem overdone, too obvious and too extensive at first do not worry. It is always better to have too much than too little and in any case it will take only a few weeks for the supports to blend in almost invisibly with the wall background.

The support system must be strong and durable and it must be firmly fixed to the wall, preferably just an inch or so away from the actual surface. This will

Many climbing plants, such as this wisteria, grow well in containers

allow some growths to go behind rather than be pinched or broken and it will also simplify the tying in of new shoots. A space between the growing greenery and the wall is also helpful to allow air to circulate. So fix your supports securely, using heavy screws or nails.

In most places it is possible to get heavy-gauge steel-mesh panels in various sizes, usually covered in heavy-duty plastic, with individual squares of about 6in. These are excellent. They can be cut to shape or size if necessary and even bent to go around a corner. They can easily be fixed in position and have a lifetime's use ahead of them.

We are all familiar with the popular wooden trellis work that has been in use for so many years and is easily and inexpensively obtainable everywhere. Treat this with one of the commercial copper-naphthenate solutions before placing it in position. This will considerably lengthen its life. Sometimes this trellis is not as strong as it seems and needs fixing to the wall in a number of places, otherwise if the wind gets under it there is a danger that it will break away. This trellis can be diamond patterned or squared according to taste. It is also quite simple to make your own from laths purchased very inexpensively, and if you wish to have a particular pattern it might be easier and more satisfactory to do it yourself than to try to adapt or cut the standard timber trellis. Again, treat it with preservative and fix it to the wall with special care before arranging your plants.

Plastic trellis, comparatively new but surely obtainable everywhere by now, is a welcome addition to the aids available to us. Following the traditional timber trellis more or less in shape and size, it is very much stronger and it will last for many years without requiring any treatment. It normally comes in green or white and is usually, though not always, accompanied by special fixing nails and spacers to keep it just off the surface of the wall. As is to be expected, it is rather more expensive in its initial purchase price than the old timber trellis, but if its life is balanced against its cost it will probably be found to be cheaper in the end. Because it is strong it needs fixing to the wall in fewer places, but these should nevertheless be sufficient to avoid any possibility of the wind blowing underneath and wrenching an entire panel off.

Some subjects grow so strongly, with long, fat and powerful shoots like roses, that they need to be tied in at fewer places than more whippy growth like that of wisteria. For these stronger growths a simpler system can be used. One which is practical, useful, very inexpensive and almost everlasting if carefully installed is the simple spacing at wide intervals, not less than 1ft and more usually 2ft, of heavy-gauge wire on firmly embedded screws. With vertical and horizontal lines of wire you get large squares of support which are quite sufficient for many plants. But if necessary support can be supplemented in a single square or a series of squares by additional wire to reduce the spacing intervals.

Panels of plastic mesh, which is sometimes available in roll form in considerable lengths, are yet another means of training and supporting wall plants. These can be useful for small areas and for some of the less active climbers, but their value for stronger growth is somewhat doubtful. They seem not to be strong enough, tending sometimes to break away from support screws or to tear in a high wind. They are useful, however, as a kind of nursery trellis on which to train young growth not yet long or strong enough to be grown on the wider-spaced mesh.

And finally there are the little special nails known as vine eyes which are still available and which have

*Parthenocissus tricuspidata*, an excellent plant for covering walls

been used since the great days of the private gardeners who used to grow a greenhouse or two of grapes and another of peaches or nectarines as well as tending an orangery and producing other fruits and vegetables for the big house. These vine eyes can be obtained either to hammer into a stone or brick wall or to screw into timber. Still another type consists of a steel nail portion with a piece of soft lead at the top which can be bent over to hold an individual stem in position.

D

# 6

# BONSAI, MINIATURE TREES AND MINIATURE GARDENS

It is interesting to speculate why the miniature has such an appeal for us. Why a ten-year-old tree should attract us simply because it is a perfect replica of a normal tree of its own type yet only one-hundredth the size is more than I can say, particularly if the miniature has been artificially gnarled and twisted to give the quite erroneous impression that it is not only of a great age but that its life has been spent under conditions of great strain and hardship.

However, we deal here with matter rather than metaphysics and what could be more material than the sinewy, not-an-ounce-to-spare grace of a well-executed specimen of bonsai? The word itself, bonsai, means in Japanese 'to plant in a shallow vessel', but both the name and the art originated in China, although the name today is known only in its Japanese version and the art was certainly brought to its highest peak in that country.

Like Japanese flower arrangement the art has its philosophical side and the various styles of design and pattern have special names and philosophical overtones. The majority of the devotees of the art in other countries are content to lump all styles together under the umbrella name of bonsai and are less interested in the different designs than in the techniques of growing and training the young trees.

There are several ways to start a bonsai collection. You can buy ready-trained trees, either young, immature and comparatively inexpensive or older, mature and costly. The best examples, like the greatest paintings, are not for sale. You can buy young seedlings from a nursery and train them yourself. You can go out into the woods and up onto the mountains and search for specimens, some of which may be both dwarfed and twisted by natural means. You can dig up and pot the little adventitious trees that appear in the garden, the little oak, horse chestnut, ash or cotoneaster that so often appear where they are not wanted. Or you can buy or collect some seed and start right from the beginning. There is no 'best' way to start, for so much will depend on your circumstances and the depth of your interest; but if you are genuinely fascinated by this art you will find that you not only buy trained trees, but also work with seedlings and seed and that you search constantly for specimens of promise which you hope to be able to grow and train into objects of beauty.

When you decide to buy an example of bonsai you will obviously go to someone with a sound reputation. If you are so new to the art that you do not know who is reputable and who is a rogue, look at the prices. Anything expensive is not necessarily good, but certainly anything cheap is bad. Any example of semi-trained bonsai must necessarily cost at least twice as much as an untrained, undwarfed tree of the same kind simply because of the extra work that has been involved. If possible go to see specimens for sale at the nursery. If you buy blind by mail order, no matter how carefully you read the advertising, no matter how closely you study the small print, you will be wasting money, time and energy.

Look for healthy growth without signs of disease or damage. Make sure that you appreciate, even enjoy, the design of the training that has been begun, for you will have to carry it on yourself. Where specimens have been pruned to achieve a certain size and shape see that the cut was neat, flush with the main stem, healing well and conducive to good shape and healthy growth in the future. See that the soil in which the tree is growing is clean, moist and healthy looking, not too muddy and apparently well drained. Where training wire is still wound around the branches look to see that it is not cutting into the bark. Check that no roots protrude above the soil level. See that the tree is well anchored in its container and that the root ball is not loose to allow rocking.

Prices of trees are related to age. Really young and untrained plants are very inexpensive, as indeed they should be, not only because they have had little work done on them but also because at that stage the plants are delicate and could very easily die. As a rule the best buys are usually trees about five or six years old, for these have had time to become established, their roots and their top growth will have been pruned and training will have started to shape the plant in the required design, and yet the prices should not yet have started to rise to the same extent as for older plants.

Two quite separate processes are required to train your young bonsai tree into the shape you have chosen. In the first the tree must gradually be dwarfed otherwise it will grow too large for its container; once it has passed a certain stage of growth it is most difficult if not impossible to bring it back again to the desired size. The dwarfing operation has already been begun by the root pruning. Now as growth gradually appears and the buds swell and develop into leaves it will be possible to get some idea of the general shape of the tree. Some of the leaves will have to be removed to help keep the tree small and obviously it will be best to remove those leaves or branches which are growing in the wrong direction. Never attempt to remove too much at one time. Instead pinch out the growing tip of a shoot or cut away a tiny branch when it appears to be growing across another or moving in the wrong direction. Try always to cut a growing shoot just above a joint so that the bud in the axil can grow and produce some fresh green foliage, even though this has in turn to be tipped as it grows to keep the shoot under control.

The pinching and pruning programme is seldom sufficient to achieve completely the desired shape. It is necessary actually to bend the young growing trunk or the developing branches. There are several ways in which this can be done, depending on the shape sought. If the young tree should bend its head in a certain direction it is a simple matter, for example, to bend the tip very gently and to tie it in position or

(*Above and facing page*) Miniature bonsai trees must always be kept under control ·pinched and trained to keep their growth in attractive balance

even to tie a small stone onto the end so that it is weighted down.

But more complex shapes demand more complicated treatments and here we turn to copper wire of a fairly heavy gauge, which is normally obtainable from an electrical store. This should be soft and easily bent yet strong enough to hold a branch in the required shape or position. The way to achieve these opposites is to heat the wire briefly over a flame or even on the heating element of an electric cooker. The idea is not to get the wire red hot but merely to heat it until it changes colour. Allowed to cool it

will be considerably more malleable than it was previously yet this quality will disappear after a brief period, which means that it will be soft and easy to bend into shape on the tree and when left for a few hours will become harder and stronger again and so hold the branch in position.

Choose carefully which tiny limbs of the tree you are going to train into position by means of this copper wire. They should not be so soft that the wire is either unnecessary or unnecessarily brutal, yet they should not be so tough and woody that they will split or break rather than bend. Use the wire only when·there is no other, easier, safer and less drastic means of achieving the desired shape, and then use it only with great care, for the operation demands delicate and agile fingers.

Wire should not normally be left in position for more than a few months, certainly not more than a year or so although much will depend on the type of tree and the toughness or softness of the bark. If it has to be removed and replaced again, try to leave a few months between successive strappings for the bark to recover.

Wiring and shaping of deciduous trees has to be done in summer when the young tree is in full growth and you can see the overall shape. Evergreen trees are best shaped in spring or autumn.

So far as the general care of bonsai is concerned, once the actual early shaping has been carried out the main thing to remember is that because the plant is growing in so small and so shallow a container it will have very little soil around its roots and this will

dry out very quickly. A happy tree growing well will need water twice a day in summer under some circumstances and an all-over spray with clean water once a day at this time will also be beneficial. Some trees will seem almost to push themselves out of the soil so that the lower trunk with its attached roots seems to stand quite clear. A normal watering may leave this area dry whereas a good spraying will help to provide moisture where it is needed.

Occasionally, perhaps once or twice a month on average throughout the year, it will be helpful to give your bonsai specimens a more thorough watering than they normally get. Fill a bucket or other large receptacle with water and then one by one place the bonsai specimens in this, letting the water cover as much of the foliage as is possible. Even

The wood of this seedling *Contoneaster horizontalis* is now strong enough to accept training

Soft copper wire is wound gently around the main stem between leaves and side shoots

though you think you have been careful with your watering programme you will be surprised to see the number and persistency of the bubbles that arise from the soil surface, showing very clearly that there are dry patches around the roots. When the bubbles have ceased to rise remove the container and set it aside to drain.

The speed with which the water drains from the soil surface in the container will give you helpful information about the state of the soil. If the excess water flows quickly through the drainage hole then the soil is in good condition, well aerated and sweet. If the water tends to hang about on the surface of the soil and penetrate it on its way to the drainage hole

Supported by the wire, the stem can now be bent to the required shape

Before being planted in its suitable permanent container the woody roots are pruned

only with apparent difficulty, and then dripping slowly and painfully, the indication is that the soil has become panned and stale and that the tree is in need of fresh soil.

The feeding of bonsai is another matter that is sometimes misunderstood. Some people believe that because we are trying to dwarf our trees they should be kept on a starvation diet. But this is not so. Naturally one would not give them the same quantity or strength of fertilisers that would be applied to a tree growing in the soil of the garden, but a little feeding keeps the plants healthy and strong while we attend to the dwarfing and the training by our pinching and pruning programme.

59

If the basic training carried out in the early years has been thorough and correct the framework of the tree will maintain this shape, but new growth will always be appearing and must not be allowed to get out of hand or it will begin to take over. So the pinching and training programme needs to be maintained to some modest extent for the whole of the life of the plant.

And now just two matters remain to be discussed briefly before we leave this fascinating subject. In the first place, do bear in mind that bonsai are not house plants. Specimens can be brought indoors for a few days at a time but should then be removed to the open air again, but even this should not be done in the coldest winter days because of the shock the plants will receive from the differences in temperature. The best place for bonsai is out in the open, but sheltered to some degree from sun, wind and rain. They look most attractive arranged on shelves or in open fronted boxes against a plain wall. Although it is not essential that they be protected from the rain it is better if they receive some shelter so that they are spared the main force of heavy rain and the continued dampness of persistent rain.

MINIATURE GARDENS

Although dwarf or miniature trees are used in the construction of miniature gardens, they are quite unlike bonsai, being both naturally dwarf and allowed to retain their natural shape. A miniature garden is a tiny version not of a complete garden but of a rock garden. It is small not because of any artificial treatment but because of the careful choice of plants of a certain size only. The garden is usually made in a stone sink or one of artificial stone as described in Chapter 3.

Size and shapes can differ widely in a group of containers as shown by these gay Mediterranean pots

61

The physical details of creating a miniature garden are simple to follow and to execute. Whether the completed garden is exquisite or an abomination depends therefore not on the skill but on the taste of the gardener, and taste is a quality impossible to impart or even to define. Certainly a sense of proportion is vital in this aspect and some knowledge of the plants used is helpful, for one must determine whether a particular plant, perhaps a little juniper, will appear in correct and happy proportion when planted in the trough or sink and in comparison with the saxifrage or sedum nearby.

The reason that most miniature gardens are actually miniature *rock* gardens is that in this line lies a particularly rich and suitable collection of plants. If one attempted to miniaturise another part of the garden could one, for example, make an attractive miniature lawn? And maintain it in condition? Or a garden pool? Without having to fill it with water two or three times a day in warm weather? Yet another advantage in the miniature rock garden is that whereas our real and full-scale rock garden must have some affinity with the local environment to look natural, the miniature is completely divorced from its surroundings. So where in the larger garden we must use limestone if we happen to live in limestone country and we must grow plants which appreciate an alkaline or neutral soil rather than one which is acid, yet for the miniature garden we are free to use any of the many different types of limestone, sandstone, granite, tufa or even marble, depending on what we can get. Neither will we have to break the bank nor our backs in the attempt.

A miniature garden should be raised from the ground for the sake of efficient drainage. It is better if it can be raised sufficiently to allow the visitor to inspect and admire without having to squat. Prob-

ably it is best raised on a wall on or beside a terrace or patio, for this way every benefit is gained. But as I said earlier, these gardens can be very heavy indeed and they should be located in their final home before planting is undertaken.

Efficient drainage is again essential for the miniature garden. The drainage hole or holes must be large enough to discourage any water from lying about on the base of the container, and the soil must be of an open texture. First cover the drainage hole with a crock or disc so that excess water can flow away freely but none of the solid contents of the sink, and so that no worms, slugs, snails or other unwanted guests can climb into the sink from the underside. There should then be a shallow layer, perhaps an inch or two depending on the depth of the container, of broken crocks, coarse shingle or other drainage material. On top of this it is helpful, though not essential, to have a layer of similar depth of coarse peat or some similar material. The purpose of this is both to prevent soil being washed down into the drainage layer and to hold and absorb water and act as a constantly moist subsoil or reservoir for the roots above.

The soil or compost can vary according to the plants we wish to grow, but a good basis can be prepared by mixing 4 parts of good fibrous loam, 2 parts of peat or leafmould, 2 parts of really coarse sand and 1 part of grit, fine gravel or the like. If any 'boulders' of stone are to be used they should be inserted as the sink is being filled with the soil mixture so that they lie as they would naturally with the greater part of their bulk underground.

If it is desired to make hills and valleys, or even to slope the entire garden down to the front, then this should be arranged at this stage, before the planting takes place. Hills and valleys can be con-

Rock garden plants, like this heather, *Erica carnea,* provide ground cover in miniature gardens

venient because it is then possible to plant on the hills certain materials with a deep root system, to give a little shelter to those plants that like it, or to place some of the little plants where rain water falling upon them is shed again and does not get trapped to set up a form of rot.

Once the plants have all been set in place (for a list of plants see Chapter 11) the surface of the soil can be covered with a quarter-inch layer of granite chippings, pea gravel or the like. This aids drainage, prevents the soil surface from drying out and gives a pleasant, smart and finished appearance.

# 7

# PLANTS IN THE AIR

Those who garden in the clouds do so for their own pleasure, and in many cases it is only their dogged determination to enjoy themselves that makes them continue, as the amount of effort needed to garden under these conditions is very considerable. Simply the fact of having to carry everything up countless stairs is enough to deter all but the most hardy souls. In addition the roof-top gardener has three special worries: weight, water and wind.

The problem of weight is the most important of all, for if the balcony or the roof is just not strong enough to carry the weight of containers, soil, plants and the immense quantities of water that they demand, then that is an end to all dreams of the hanging gardens of Brooklyn or wherever. However, buildings today are immensely strong and fortunately container-grown plants have their weight spread fairly evenly over a wide area, so the probability is that, within reason, some sort of gardening is possible. But every gardener in the clouds would be wise to make quite sure that in his renting agreement there exists no clause specifically debarring him from growing plants and if he has the least doubt on the question of safety it is his duty to the community to check with the owners of the property or with an independent expert to make quite sure that his activities will be safe.

Before he begins to garden he should also have a close look at his site and see that it is well and safely drained, that the flooring surface is free from cracks or holes and that it adjoins surrounding walls tightly and without gaps. Where there is risk that water or debris will fall onto or blow into nearby property or premises, whether these are below or at the same level, then he will either have to erect some kind of safety barrier or exercise great care with his gardening activities so as to ensure that they do no damage. Above all he must be certain that his plants, his soil, his tools, are all secure against the unexpected gust of wind which could send any of them flying, to hurt or damage people or property. Dry soil soon becomes dust and this can be a considerable nuisance to neighbours, particularly if the baby is asleep on the balcony or if the washing has just been hung out to dry.

We already know that plants in containers need a great deal of water because the limited amount of soil around their roots dries out so quickly. So, if humanly possible, fix up a piped water supply on the roof or the balcony. Often this can be led through a window or doorway from kitchen or bathroom although this tends to be a nuisance and can cause dirt and damage if there is some lack of care. It is a justifiable expense, then, to have a standpipe installed at some convenient spot outside or so nearly outside that it can be employed easily and safely.

Watering must be carried out to excess, which means that water will be running away from the drainage holes of the containers and onto the roof. Some of this water will carry with it tiny portions of soil. When this is allowed to flow to waste it not only diminishes the amount of soil remaining but also builds up until entrances to drainpipes, perhaps even the drains themselves, become blocked. In view of this some sort of a soil trap should be installed, nothing elaborate but sufficient to collect the soil before it enters the drain, so that it can be replaced. It is most important that the drainage system should be kept quite clear, or very considerable damage can be caused. Individual drip trays for the various containers may be a luxury but they do away with a number of anxieties. They can at the same time save money, for because frequent watering is so necessary it is equally necessary to feed plants more often than usual, and excess water can be collected in drip pans and later returned to the plants; this will also return to them much of the liquid fertiliser that has been leached out of the soil.

One further thing about watering needs to be said. Because so much water is required there exists the temptation to install some kind of an automatic watering system, the choice obviously being governed by the area to be watered, the number of plants and containers, their position and a number of other related matters. An oscillating or revolving lawn spray system is suitable for certain roof gardens; for others it might be possible merely to prop a hosepipe

securely in the position required to send a steady spray over the plants. Unfortunately any unsupervised watering depends not only on the infallibility of the system employed but also on the absence of any gust of wind which could so easily send a drift of spray in the wrong direction. The only really safe form of automatic watering is a trickle system and this can quite easily and inexpensively be installed, particularly on a balcony or where the number of containers to be kept moist is not too large.

The simplest form of trickle or drip watering consists of a réservoir of water from which leads one or more small-gauge rubber or plastic tubes. These are perforated at intervals, or possibly fitted with little adjustable nozzles, to allow water from the reservoir to drip slowly onto the soil of each container where they have been placed. Although somewhat unsightly, this system in one or other of its forms can be a great help in warm weather.

Closely allied with the problems of weight and water is the question of floor surface. Today this is usually some form of bituminous compound, or perhaps slimmer and lighter versions of the familiar paving slab. Sheet lead is seldom seen now, and bituminous paper is only for temporary covering or for shed or outhouse. This floor surface must be able to withstand extremes of weather, frost and snow and summer baking.

Roof surfaces and balcony floors get very hot indeed when the sun shines and this heat softens bituminous compounds so that hard edges tend to press into the softened material. This is particularly the case where considerable thrust is exerted on a small area, as for example when a container stands on legs. If the weight were more evenly spread over the surface there would be much less penetration. For this reason it is always advisable to stand all containers on some intermediate surface, flat and wide-spreading. A plank or block of wood is excellent, for this is impermeable, resilient enough to take the weight of the container safely, yet just soft enough not to press too hard on the roof surface.

So as containers are essential and as weight is a problem, we must have a look at lightweight containers of various types to choose the best for the roof and balcony. Stone, imitation stone, concrete, lead, terracotta, pottery and other clays are out because of the problem of weight, and even timber and asbestos are really too heavy. The answer really lies in various forms of plastic and fibreglass.

As with so many things the better article is usually the more expensive, but there are exceptions and to buy on the recommendation of price alone would be stupid. Examine the containers available to you and try to compare them with the weight, consistency, thickness and flexibility of the average little plastic flowerpot in which you buy a primula or a pelargonium from a market or street stall. The container you choose must be heavier, more solid, thicker-walled and less flexible if it is to carry out its task efficiently over a long period. Some of the thinner plastic materials tend to disintegrate under the effect of the ultra-violet rays in the sun's spectrum and some also will crack or shatter if dropped, or even if bumped or hit accidentally with a spade or trowel.

Regardless of the horizontal size of your container make sure that it contains sufficient vertical depth to allow a plant to grow in it for long periods, particularly if you intend to grow a tree or shrub. For colours a soft green or a white or grey are always suitable and some sort of uniformity is to be preferred to a firework display of dramatic hues. The hard edge at the top of containers is always ugly so try to disguise or soften it, preferably with one or

66

The climbing *clematis jackmanii* likes artificial shade on a roof area

two trailing plants which will grow over this edge and cascade down the side. Plants trailing down the sides of a container fulfil another purpose too: their growth shades the container when it is in the full sun, thus keeping the roots pleasantly cool and reducing the transpiration of moisture from the pot.

The sun can, in fact, be a real problem on a roof garden because under certain circumstances there may be no shelter at all and the hot sun shining all day on a roof which under normal conditions absorbs the heat can so heat up containers, soil, roots and plants that they wilt and perhaps even die. Yet on a balcony the opposite may be the case. Here it is possible that the sun never enters and that the plants growing there must live forever in the shade.

Steps can be taken to ease the difficulties caused by over-exposure to the sun. We have already seen that trailers growing over the sides of the containers can protect their contents to some extent from the worst of the heat, and here one would use something tough, woody and perhaps even fleshy which can absorb the sun's heat safely, perhaps one of the ivies or succulents. We can also orientate the garden, shape and design it, so that the worst of the sun will do the least damage. It may be possible to grow one or two taller trees or shrubs to the south with the intention that they should provide a certain amount of shade. It is also possible to grow a tough and vigorous climber in a large tub on the south and take its trails up supports to travel across much of the area of the roof along firmly fixed wires or cords. The rampant *Polygonum bilderdyckia baldschuanicum*, as long as its name but considerably more attractive with its trailing stems and its foam of off-white flowers, is particularly suitable. It grows happily in a large tub and will put on several feet of growth in each of its many trails in a single season. It and many other

similar climbers will give a soft and dappled shade, far more beneficial than a darker one.

Artificial shade can be given to the roof area fairly easily and inexpensively but only if the wind allows. Rush or split bamboo matting can be bought cheaply in rolls and stretched over just the same kind of wire supports that might be used to grow the polygonum just mentioned or a clematis or other climber. Only certain areas need shade of this kind and a careful watch of the sun and shade pattern will indicate the best place to position the matting so that it gives the greatest benefit.

The heat of the actual roof surface can be appreciably reduced by changing its colour. Normally it will be a dark grey-black in colour, a hue notoriously able to absorb the greatest possible quantity of heat. If we can change the colour to white or to some lighter tint then we will be using the roof as a reflector rather than as an absorber and the actual roof surface temperature will be lower. It might be possible to paint the surface with a special kind of paint and this might accept changes of temperature, all kinds of weather conditions and the constant inevitable trickle and drip of water, but I cannot imagine that it would also accept the passage of feet and the scraping of heavy containers along its surface without showing some sign of strain.

Some of the special stone paints can be used on walls or parapets where a change of colour is desired. This can be particularly helpful where there is a shade problem. If a container and its plants are in deep shade all day and every day one cannot expect the more vivid and enjoyable plants to grow well. Yet if the nearby wall or floor is painted white or near-white to accept and reflect the greatest possible amount of light then a considerable difference will be seen in the growth of these plants. It is also possible, where this seems necessary, to install artificial reflectors, possibly on a temporary basis and capable of easy removal, to take the greatest possible advantage of the sun.

It may have been noticed that particular attention has been paid not just to growing plants high up on our urban buildings but to growing them *well*. The reason for this is that in the ground-level earth garden plants are easier to grow and they grow better; one or two plants which have failed for one reason or another will hardly be noticed for the plethora of others which surround and almost engulf it. Yet on the roof or balcony a single faded petunia or pansy is instantly spotted and a tub or trough with a few tired pelargoniums in it so lowers the tone of the whole area that even the gorgeous passion flower growing on the wall nearby will fail to redeem it.

Some discipline and some grooming will be required if the containers are not to get out of hand. Each day plants should be inspected, flowers dead-headed, withered leaves removed, new shoots tied in to stake or other support, particular and perfect flowers cut for indoor decoration, and where necessary leaves cleaned from city grime. Evergreens in particular (rhododendrons are an example) will collect a thick coat of sooty dirt which will not be removed with ordinary rain or with watering. The leaves may have to be wiped individually, but by so doing the whole appearance of the plant will be immeasurably improved and at the same time its future health assured.

One of the reasons for plants getting dirty on roof-tops is that they get spattered with dusty soil from the containers. Every time it rains, or every time we water, a little of the soil mixture is lost. This is wasteful both of material and of time and fortunately

E

there is something we can do about it.

The soil or soil mixture we use is largely dictated by what we can get, but in many cases, balancing cost against weight, it is found that the best buy is a light although comparatively expensive no-soil compost. These peaty no-soil composts are very fine in texture, almost powdery. This texture is important for it allows the entry of plenty of air. If the mixture is compressed then it loses much of its undoubted efficiency. Yet when loose and powdery it tends both to dry out very quickly and to blow about in the slightest breeze. When water is applied it compacts slightly and over months of use its level will undoubtedly drop and will have to be topped up. As stated earlier one of its many advantages is that drainage is so sharp that no special drainage layer needs to be installed. We can take advantage of this fact and use the drainage material we have at the top instead of the base of the container, as a mulch instead of a drainage layer. It wants only half an inch of pea gravel scattered lightly over the surface of the no-soil compost to hold it down so that it does not blow about and at the same time to help conserve the moisture that it holds. This gravel or other drainage material will not affect in any way the flow of water through the compost.

There are several alternatives to gravel or similar material. Granite chippings give a decorative finish and even larger pebbles will do the job satisfactorily so long as they are not so heavy that they sink into or compact the soft surface. Any of these materials, it will be understood, should be applied only after any seeds have germinated or any plants have been inserted into the soil, for otherwise they will tend to discourage tender and immature growth.

Fortunately there is little weed problem on a roof or balcony, for even if we use unsterilised soil in which to grow our plants we necessarily pay such close attention to every container that individual weeds can easily be plucked out as they appear. But another problem we do have on many city roofs and even on some balconies is the visitation of city birds, largely sparrows and pigeons. It is only natural that they will visit every source of natural greenery that they can find, but their destructive pecking at some of the plants and their habit of taking dust baths in our precious compost need to be discouraged. There is no real way to keep them off the plants except by stringing black cotton just above or by using one of the chemical deterrents, but the use of a gravel, pebble or granite mulch will keep them off the surface of the soil.

# 8

# RAISED BEDS AND PUDDLE-POTS

One of the many obvious advantages of container gardening is that the container can be placed anywhere you like, at different heights as well as in different places. It would be crazy to lift a container above head height except where it can be seen at a distance and even chest height would make it awkward both to see and to tend. But when a container is placed so that it is about waist high the plants it contains are easier to see, easier to smell and admire and also easier to tend.

Waist-high gardening is also ideal for those who through age, accident or illness cannot bend to do their gardening at ground level. At this height they can plant and weed from a chair or even a wheelchair, or they can stand with one hand on familiar stick while the other is used to pluck out an invasive weed. In some cases the incapacitated can even perch on the broad side of an elevated garden and carry out simple operations from that position.

This last suggestion presupposes not so much a raised container as one which is built into a raised portion of the garden, patio or terrace. Many terrace walls, in fact, are made more or less on this principle, where in effect there are two walls with an interior trough, planted up as a rule with bright plants to make a colourful band along the top of the wall. The actual soil container is seldom more than about 1ft deep and this rests on top of the otherwise solid or core-packed wall. Drainage holes should be provided every few feet otherwise the water will tend to weep from the sides through the stone or brick and so stain and dampen the sides of the walls. If the wall has a rubble-packed centre instead of being solid, the excess moisture can drain away through this.

On a more ambitious scale a whole flowerbed can be raised to waist level and this can be as long as liked. For the sake of convenience in tending it, particularly for the disabled, a bed of this nature should not be more than about 2ft wide if it is planted against a wall and 4ft wide if it is free standing so that it can be reached from both sides. The most convenient height is about 2ft to 2ft 6in.

If a flowerbed is to be raised to waist level then it must be quite secure and there must be no danger that the top or sides will crumble and give way. For this reason the building of raised beds is a somewhat

lengthy business. The easiest and one of the most foolproof methods is to use prefabricated paving stones, square or rectangular. A convenient size, though very heavy, is 3ft × 2ft. Much will depend on the size of the bed and adaptation of these directions is a simple matter.

Having decided on the size of the bed, let us take, for example, one 4ft square, the ground should be excavated about 6in to 1ft deep to this size. The paving slabs should be stood on edge around the perimeter, the long sides being vertical. Spend some time making sure that they fit well together and are at the same height and angle. Hardcore rammed around the bases of the slabs should hold them securely in position but if there is any doubt they can be concreted in. The interior of the square should then have rubble, coarse ash, half bricks and any other filling and draining matter dumped in place until within about a foot or so of the top of the paving slabs.

If soil were to be filled in at this stage there is no doubt that much of it would trickle through the drainage layers and thus be lost, at the same time helping to choke the drainage. For this reason it is wise to insert some sort of a barrier between infilling and soil. One useful material would be turf, perhaps the very turf that was removed to make the hole in the first place. If the turves are laid over the drainage stones, grass downwards and closely together, then soil placed on top will not be able to sift through. If no turf is available peat bricks can be used in exactly the same way. These have the advantage of soaking up water and so except in particularly dry and arid times they form a cool and moist base for the soil above. And failing both these materials as a barrier it is worth spreading over the stones some coarse sacking, even an old blanket or shirt, to keep

Beds raised on paving are containers in the widest sense of the word. These are great space winners if they are made to follow the perimeter of the area. Tubs and other types of free-standing containers can complement the beds. Apart from their decorative use, these tubs can usefully hold those plants which need protection in winter

the soil from drifting through.

The type of soil used to fill in at the top will depend mainly on what you intend to grow. The plot is so well drained that with a really gritty soil it would be possible to grow cacti successfully yet it is equally possible to use a soil mixture rich with peat or leafmould that will support even such moisture lovers as primulas. Remember that after it has first been filled the soil will tend to settle for a week or two, so if there is time it will be worth waiting a little before planting or sowing, and top up to the required level first.

The walls of a raised garden such as this are bound to look somewhat stark, so grow trailers around the sides to hang down and cover some of the bare cement. It will be inadvisable to grow any plants at the foot of the paving slabs as this will be an area where the feet will be sure to tread while the bed is being tended.

A considerably more attractive finish can be obtained by making the walls of the bed not from austere paving slabs but from walling stone. A dry-stone wall, one without mortar between the courses, is much more attractive to look at and has the added advantage that little plants can be induced to grow in the cracks and crevices so that the entire structure is clothed, as it were, in growing plants.

It is probably advisable to set a wall of this nature on a solid concrete foundation but it certainly is not necessary. What is essential is that the wall should have a slight but definite inward 'batter', which is to say that the sides of the wall should lean very slightly inwards, for by doing this they support each other, water drains into the wall (rather than out of it) and the stones are well 'bonded' by the soil inside the bed. It is easier and safer to fill in the centre as work proceeds rather than wait until

the bed has been completed. Use the same kind of filling materials.

Lay the first course of stones around the perimeter, either on the foundation, bedding the stones firmly into the concrete, or onto level ground, making quite sure that each stone is as firm, secure and level as you can get it. Lay the second course on top of the first with the outer edge sloping very slightly inwards towards the centre. Use a little sifted soil to bed the stones one on the other and between each other so that they fit snugly and firmly. On occasions and where convenient leave a gap 2–3in square and place a little plant there which will grow and fill the space. Stonecrops and house leeks are excellent for positions such as this where they may have to go dry or almost dry for comparatively long periods.

Continue in the same way until the required height has been reached. The wall should be thicker at the base than at the top and if it is intended that the top should be broad, broad enough for sitting on for example, then allowance will have to be made for this at the beginning and it will be essential that the top few courses are firmly cemented into position rather than just left with soil between them.

Although the space at the top in which the plants grow is technically a container the soil level should not be below the edges as it generally is in other containers. In fact raised beds of this kind look best if the soil forms a slight mound at the centre. The reason for the gap between soil level and rim in other containers is to facilitate watering. With a raised bed there is a sufficient quantity of soil so that far less frequent watering is needed than with a mere tub or trough.

A rather lower bed can be built most successfully using peat bricks instead of stone, but in exactly the same way. They do not have the same stability or

If there exists little room for free-standing containers, there often are little corners and other areas which can be converted to hold plants. On the shingle, this bed is just one brick high but it is deep enough for bulbs and small bedding plants

strength as stone so they cannot be built so high, but once the raised bed has been completed and planted the peat bricks begin to settle in and become firm and solid. The advantage here is not only in appearance but that by filling with an acid soil it is possible to grow many peat-loving and lime-hating plants otherwise denied to us.

Whatever plants are used bear in mind that because the bed is raised it will have lost just a little of the protection that a ground-level bed might expect to receive. So do not use any plants that grow too tall. Stakes would look ugly indeed. But there are plenty of low-growing plants of all kinds, from bright annuals to perennials and shrubs, that will look most attractive in raised beds. Simply because the plants are growing at waist level instead of on the ground and we can thus see them more closely than we are accustomed to do, the smaller plants such as alpines seem to have a particular attraction and it is a happy coincidence that they are also particularly suited to growing under these conditions. They do not, however, give quite the same dramatic effect from further away, from the house for example, that we might get if the raised bed were planted with brilliant pelargoniums or even with dwarf azaleas and bulbs. On the other hand every raised bed can be tailor-made for the plants it is to hold and for this reason it is pleasant to have several of them in the garden, preferably in formal positions rather than dotted randomly about the place.

### PUDDLE-POTS

We can grow many plants in a strange halfway world, neither in soil in a container nor in the water of a pool but in what are called 'puddle-pots' and by a system invented, I believe, by my wife Violet

Stevenson. It is only fair to say at once that this system is applicable to outdoor gardening only in the summer or in climates which are kind and gentle, although there is no reason why the container bearing the plants should not be brought into the shelter and warmth of the home when colder weather descends.

The idea is to grow certain plants and certain cuttings in a container filled with pebbles and water, in a way a form of hydroponics. The advantages of the process are that plants can be inserted and removed with the minimum of fuss and that cuttings of many plants can be struck this way and subsequently left to grow where they have taken root or removed and planted elsewhere.

The puddle-pot can be any size but is best relatively small and shallow. It should not have drainage holes. To plant, half fill the container with pebbles of any size from pea to golf ball and preferably fairly uniform for ease of handling. If young plants are to be inserted remove them from pot or box and wash the roots clear of soil, doing this very gently under running water. Spread the roots on the pebbles already in the container and place more pebbles in position to hold the roots in place and the plant stem vertical. Repeat the process with other plants if there is space and then top up with water. The water will need replenishing frequently, perhaps even more than once a day during hot weather, and this should not be forgotten. Once a week or so add some general fertiliser.

Cuttings are taken in the normal way. It would be necessary to go into considerable detail to deal fully with the subject so those who require further information should seek it elsewhere. On the other hand it is so easy, so quick and so inexpensive to try that simple experiment may indeed be the best way

The sword-like acorus, cream and green, will grow happily in water or at the moist water's edge

to find out. The cutting, hardwood or softwood, should merely be inserted into the water and pebbles and left there. If the method is going to work then root formation will begin in a week or two and by the end of a few weeks the roots will have developed sufficiently to allow the new plant to be removed and potted up separately. If the pot is to be brought indoors at any time it may be helpful to place in the lower layers of pebbles a few nuggets of charcoal to absorb any offensive odours that come from the stagnant water. Outside these will not be noticed.

The size of the plants growing in the puddle-pot and the rate of growth will depend mainly on the amount of food they are given. It is possible to grow miniature coleus and antirrhinums, for example, which will make charming indoor decorations, and equally it is possible to grow them huge, lush and flamboyant for exhibition and admiration in the garden.

77

# 9

# LUXURY LOVERS

Although we do not intend here to enter the wide and wonderful world of house plants, our container label will allow us into the halfway world of the sun lounge, the garden extension room, that area which is neither house nor garden but an extension of each and a link between both. All trees and most shrubs will normally be denied to us here but otherwise the good light, the protective shelter, the luxuriant warmth and the access to the outdoor air mean that we can grow many plants here which we could not grow in the garden, and we can so improve the growth patterns of others that they seem almost unrecognisable.

The very qualities of the location, however, also set some problems, for the room is as heavily windowed as possible, for obvious reasons, and although this interior light is enjoyed by the plants we may grow the sheer area of window space cuts down severely the possibilities of growing and displaying plants. Climbers will cover the windows and cut down the light entering. So will any taller plants and even small plants grown on tables or shelving. So we have to evolve a new style of indoor decoration if we are to make the most of our plants and of the building in which they are to be housed.

We must also be realistic about the benefits that are brought to us in a building of this character. There will be sharp temperature changes between day and night and although ventilation and heating may serve to some extent to create a more even temperature, we will have to keep these temperature differences very much in mind when we decide what plants to display.

Because this room is still primarily a part of the living quarters the atmosphere must be comfortable for normal human activity, which means that it will be drier and less humid than is generally enjoyed by plants. During the daytime in the warmer months a softer, moister atmosphere can be provided by increasing the ventilation and opening the room to outdoors, but this may not be practicable or advisable during winter, when the combination of sun and artificial heating may dry the air to dangerous levels. It will not be possible to damp down the floor as one might do in a greenhouse or even in a conservatory, nor will it normally be possible to spray plants to the extent that we would like.

In a room such as this it will not be advisable to use any particularly large containers. We may not have to limit ourselves entirely to the traditional clay or plastic flowerpots, but we will almost certainly grow considerable numbers of our plants in these and because no pots of this kind should ever be used in any room without a saucer or stand of some kind, it will be possible to use large waterproof plant trays on which to stand them. If the floor of these is covered with pea gravel or some such substance this can be kept permanently wet, thus providing a certain reservoir of moisture at the base of the plant pots and at the same time adding appreciably to the general humidity of the atmosphere.

If there is space it is most helpful in a room of this nature to make a special feature which will not only look attractive but will at the same time provide extra humidity for both summer and winter. An example of such a feature would be a large round or rectangular tray-like container on the floor. This could hold in one corner almost any attractive and tall plant, probably a shrub, possibly a conifer. The remainder of the surface would be strewn with pebbles or shells kept constantly moist, perhaps even with a small indoor fountain playing over them.

There is no reason why one should not install a miniature pool on the floor, preferably heated and controlled by an electric thermostat, where tropical fish can swim and miniature waterlilies can grow. Once again this would provide a great deal of the humidity that the room requires and at the same time create a charming focal point of interest for everyone.

One of the great advantages of the garden room is that it enables one to make and to enjoy some of those special and intimate plant arrangements that are the test of the skill and the taste of the gardener and simultaneously the pleasure of the artist. The creation of a plant arrangement probably calls for even more skill than the building of a flower arrange-

A fine ensemble of house plants decorate a garden room. If regularly fed and watered and given adequate humidity such plants will grow happily for years. On the other hand, plants still in their individual pots can be arranged in a more temporary decoration

ment, for a further element has been added, that of time. For as a rule the flower arrangement is known to be fleeting; the flowers last a few days only and although they certainly develop during this period the changes they undergo are unlikely significantly to alter their sizes, shapes or colours. But some plant arrangements will last for years, during which time all the plants contained in their small world can change in size, colour and shape according to maturity and even throughout the year according to season.

PLANT ARRANGEMENTS IN THE SUN LOUNGE
There are two main ways of creating a plant arrangement. You can knock the plants from their pots and plant them all together in the soil of the container, or you can plunge the plants complete with their pots in the soil. The latter is the safer method so long as the container is large enough, for it means that should you turn out to be wrong in your judgement of the suitable juxtaposition of certain plants then it is a relatively simple matter to remove one pot and replace it with another. It also means that if a certain plant should fail to make the grade and should die or even look poorly, then again this can be removed quite easily. The important thing is that the container must be deep enough so that each of the plant pots can be plunged in without the rim showing. This gives the impression that each plant is growing in the soil of the container rather than still in its own individual pot.

In the days, not really so far distant, when all flowerpots were of clay or terracotta, it was much easier to make a successful arrangement of plunged pots than it is today when only plastic pots are to be found. The terracotta pots were obligingly able to absorb moisture through their sides as well as

80

For a frost-free site, or for a garden room, there are many handsome succulent plants which will grow for years and call for little care. Architecturally beautiful as plants, as they mature, many species produce strange, interesting and beautiful flowers

Bromeliads are both handsome and long-lived. Diverse in colour, they call for little care, growing best where the air can be kept a little moist. Tree branches and driftwood, well covered with moss, make good hosts for epiphytic plants

their bases, so when they were plunged in a soil mixture the roots were contained and restrained in their pots but otherwise temperatures and moisture contents were more or less identical with the soil mixture surrounding them. But a modern plastic pot has an impervious wall and its only contact with the outer soil is either through the relatively small drainage holes in the base of the pot or through any soil that may rise above the rim of the pot. This means that watering is a little more difficult and a somewhat finer judgement is necessary. With a terracotta pot it was possible to water either the surrounding soil or the soil in the individual pots knowing full well that one would so influence the other that in a matter almost of minutes there would be an average moisture throughout the entire container and all of its plants. But in using plastic pots it is necessary to water every individual plant to make quite sure that it receives the moisture it needs, for it is quite possible to have a container soil apparently moist and hospitable holding a pot of compost so dry that the roots are shrinking away from the soil. This is still another reason, quite apart from the aesthetic, why the container soil should cover the pot completely and overlap its top, for thus some of the moisture in the top soil can seep down.

In view of these facts it is helpful to choose certain special qualities for the soil in our mother container. It should not be so sharply drained as is usual in containers and it should be particularly retentive of moisture. Peat is the answer, and a richly moist peat is probably the best medium we can choose for these circumstances.

But there is still another matter to consider with these indoor gardens. Out of doors it is important that containers have good drainage and efficient drainage holes, but indoors this is less important. The thing is that when they are outside the amount of water they receive cannot be controlled, and in periods of heavy or prolonged rain a container may receive so much water that unless the drainage is efficient the soil may become completely waterlogged. But indoors all watering is done by hand and can be carefully controlled so that there should be no danger of waterlogging, although special care must be taken if the container has no drainage holes.

We have seen earlier that air around a plant's roots is as important as moisture and that this air is usually provided in the watering process; when the water courses through the soil in a container and rushes out at the base it drags air down after it from the top. So in view of the importance of air and the fact that this is how it is provided, it is apparent that we must maintain the flow of water downwards by some means even when there are no drainage holes. In the first place we should use a soil or compost which is naturally open and contains large numbers of air spaces yet which is also water retentive, normally one with a high proportion of peat or leafmould. We should also provide in the base of the container a drainage system which attracts the flow of water downwards almost to the same extent as drainage holes. So in the base of the container we place a good layer of broken crocks, of clinker, of pebbles or anything that will allow the immediate passage of water. This will attract the water downwards and force air in from the top.

This drainage layer in the base of the container will only be effective so long as it is not filled with water. When this happens it loses its capability to pull water downwards. It is evident then that the drainage layer should be as deep and efficient as is allowed by the depth of the container. And equally it follows that watering should be carried out with the intention of leaving the drainage area with as little water in it as possible, this vacant space providing, in effect, a safeguard against possible over-watering at any time.

In practice, however, the drainage space at the base of the container nearly always contains a certain amount of water. This sometimes gets stale, when it can produce unpleasant odours in the room and perhaps even toxic gases around the plant roots, so it is wise not only to avoid excess water in the base but to take steps to neutralise any gases which might be produced. This is done very simply by incorporating in the drainage material a few nuggets of charcoal, which has the capacity to absorb smells. It costs very little and weighs almost nothing so a few pieces should always be used in the drainage layer of all indoor containers.

BOTTLE GARDENS

A good drainage layer together with a few pieces of charcoal is also necessary for a bottle garden or one made in a glass candy or kitchen jar or similar container. The growing of plants like this is not particularly difficult so long as a few simple rules are observed and a few simple precautions taken. A bottle garden can last for years and require a total during this time of only a few minutes attention, so it is worth spending a little time on it at the beginning.

The first essential is a bottle or jar which is free from all cracks and chips and which is meticulously clean, both inside and outside. It is simple enough to clean the outside but where it is impossible to insert the hand because of the size of the opening, cleaning the inside is a different matter. One of the best ways of doing it is to put in two or three handfuls of sand and gravel and a pint of water. This can be rocked and swished about and will gently scratch off any surface dirt. Make sure that it is emptied away thoroughly by several rinses of clean water. It is always best where possible to use rain water rather than water from the tap or faucet, for lime and chemicals in 'artificial' water tends to leave marks, smears and stains on the glass. After the water has been emptied away the interior should be swabbed dry if possible or otherwise left to dry naturally. It is important that the interior is not only spotlessly clean but that it is also bone dry.

Before describing the process of filling the bottle with plants it might be helpful to describe one or two of the special tools that may be necessary. It will be obvious that where the container has a mouth sufficiently large to permit the entry of a hand there will be no problem in planting, but where this is not so certain special tools will be required and these can be as many and as varied as your own ingenuity can devise. The following suggestions describe just a few improvisations that have been found helpful in the past and which are simple to make from materials readily available in most homes.

First some approximation of a spade will be necessary and the most easily obtained substitute is probably a spoon, its size depending once again on the size of the aperture. This spoon should be lashed securely to a thin cane, long enough easily to reach the base of the container through the hole at the top. Another essential is some kind of rammer or firmer of the soil and a good tool here can be made from a cotton reel with a long cane thoroughly wedged into the central hole. It is always helpful to have some means of picking up a fallen leaf or moving a plant from one position to another and here chopsticks may possibly provide an answer. Alternatively it is possible to use a pair of long thin canes in the same way, but you have to be pretty skilled to do this successfully. Simpler, although less effective, is a

tool made by strapping two or more long, heavy and strong pins to the end of a cane so that they can be used to impale the fallen leaf or to pierce the stem of a plant and so move it to another position. Sometimes it is necessary to use more than one implement at the same time, as for example when a little plant is being held in one position while compost is carefully drawn over its roots. The canes used must therefore be slim enough to allow for this, and the implements at the end of the canes should be attached so securely that there is no danger of them falling off. Should this happen it will probably be found that the only way to remedy the situation is to empty the bottle or carboy completely and begin all over again.

One further tool is a simple funnel or chute down which the drainage material and compost can be slid into the base of the container. It is not absolutely necessary but it is helpful. If compost, for example, has to be inserted spoonful by spoonful the task will take so long and be so boring that mistakes will almost certainly be made, resulting in a fall of compost in the wrong position or dirty marks on the side of the jar. A simple chute can be made out of newspaper or cardboard. It should project some way down into the interior of the container so that when it is moved about the compost can be deposited wherever it is required.

The drainage layer should be the first to travel down the chute into the interior, but take care. If pebbles or gravel of any weight are to be used it is possible that they may crack the base. In this case first send down just a small amount of peat or some similar soft material which will cushion the fall of the stones and prevent them doing any damage. Then slip the drainage material down the chute knowing that it can do no harm. Allow at least a

2in layer, and although perhaps not strictly necessary in this case a few pieces of charcoal can do nothing but good.

Before inserting the compost decide exactly what plants are to be used in the container and where they are to be placed. It is perhaps helpful to arrange the plants more or less in position in relation to one another before they are actually placed in the bottle. This will indicate how they will look from certain angles. It is usually best to have a front and a back to the container rather than hope so to arrange the plants that they look at their best from any angle. It is also helpful to have a slight downward slope from the back to the front, to show up plants to advantage.

Any slope should of course be arranged before the plants are to be inserted. If it is to be a simple slope then after inserting the drainage layer merely lean the container over until the stones achieve the required incline and the soil can then be placed on top of it. If a more complex hillock is desired then it may be necessary to move the chute about to achieve the required contours.

The soil or compost used should be sharply drained, containing some, but not too much, peat or leafmould, granular rather than powdery and without the addition of any fertiliser. It is a good idea to cover the drainage layer with slightly moistened compost to a depth of, say, three inches or so and then to pour dry compost on top of this for about another inch. Then the little planting hole or trench made for the roots will go down into moistened soil, which is just what the roots need. The drier soil on the surface helps to conserve the moisture below and only gradually absorbs it after the last of the plants has been put in position.

The plants themselves will almost certainly have been grown in pots so it will be necessary to knock them from the pots and expose their roots before they are dropped through the hole in the container onto the soil beneath. In some cases the root ball may appear to be too large to go through this hole, in which case some of the soil can be gently teased away from the hair roots or even washed away under a gently running tap. It should be possible in most cases to hold the little plant by the upper foliage, insert the roots through the hole and then swing it gently until when dropped it falls neatly into the prepared hole. The roots can then be covered by means of the spoon and the soil firmed down on them by the cotton reel. When all the plants have been placed in position insert a stone or two or perhaps a twig or a piece of bark to add to the decorative effect, or perhaps build up a terrace or upper level, although of course none of this is necessary and it may even be redundant when the plants have grown a little and hidden the soil in which they are growing.

When all the planting is complete the glass bottle will probably have become slightly soiled on both inner and outer surfaces. It is a simple enough matter to wipe down the outside and the best way now to clean the inner surface is to insert a garden spray, preferably the kind with an angled head, and gently spray the inner walls with rain water, just enough to rinse down any dross into the soil surface but no more. The soil should be as dry as it is possible to keep it.

Leave the mouth or opening of the container without any obstruction as the very slight amount of air that enters will help prevent any damping off. Keep the bottle in a cool and slightly shaded place for the first week or two until the plants recover from the shock of planting and begin to grow away. Water very lightly and very seldom, probably not

F

more frequently than once every two months or so, but this depends of course on such factors as temperature and light. Remove with your spike any leaves that fall, any flowers that fade or even any plants that die, and keep the soil surface as clean as possible from any debris that might serve to introduce or spread disease. You will probably find that in the mornings a slight mist of condensation appears on the inner surface of the glass. This will disappear during the day and it gives a rough indication that the plants do not require watering. When this condensation no longer appears it suggests that a little water is needed, although this will have to be confirmed by your own observations. Do not feed. The plants should grow slowly and not too large and if you give them fertiliser they will soon out-grow their container. Never allow the bottle to stand for more than a few minutes in direct sunshine, for through glass this can raise the temperature inside the confined space to dangerous levels. If you find that some of the plants tend to turn to-wards the light source after a time, move the bottle to the other side of the window or turn it every other day so that all plants get the same quantity of light. Never let the bottle stand too close to the source of any heat.

Many types of glass vessel can be employed for the same kind of indoor garden and much the same advice applies for all, although the larger the opening at the top the more water can be given. Outsize 'brandy balloons' are popular and here, and in similar containers, one or more of the plants can be allowed in time to appear through the opening, which gives a somewhat greater scope when plant-ing. Some of these containers are made of tinted glass and for this reason may require rather stronger light than should normally be allowed.

86

## HANGING BASKETS

So far in the garden room we have considered only containers which can stand on the floor, on tables or on some kind of shelving around the walls. But this is the place where hanging baskets look very much at home, either in the room itself or on the outer walls or doorway. A hanging basket can be one of the most charming and delightful of plant arrangements and it can also look one of the most poor and pathetic. The difference may lie in the plants used, the location of the basket or the compost in which the plants are growing, but the most likely reason is that one basket is not receiving sufficient water. Far too many hanging baskets are planted up and hung in position and only then it is found that to lower them for watering is a difficult task indeed and to water them in situ is almost impossible.

The answer to this problem can be a simple step-ladder, but it is perhaps annoying to have to bring this out once a day in the summer or even more often. When installing the hanging baskets it is usually possible, instead of hanging them on a hook, to attach them to a stout rope or piece of wire and to suspend this from a pulley. This will enable the basket to be lowered quite easily for watering. An alternative is to strap the end of the hose to a long, strong cane so that it can be lifted up to the hanging basket. Of these alternatives the pulley system is probably the more satisfactory.

It is, indeed, the problem of watering hanging baskets that has led to the introduction of new types of basket in various plastics and usually incorporating some kind of reservoir which cuts down the necessity for such frequent watering. It must be admitted, however, that these newer types do not have the unsophisticated charm of a well-planted and well-maintained basket of the older kind and if this is

41

Hanging baskets help fill a porch with colour to present a gay and welcoming face to the visitor correctly made and planted-up it should be possible to maintain it in good condition without too much strain. One helpful little trick is merely to place a saucer or shallow dish in the base of the basket before planting. This will serve to catch some of the drips, but even more important it will act as a reservoir and cut down the amount of water required.

Most hanging baskets are about 12–18in diameter and 6–8in deep. They can be made from galvanised wire, plastic-coated wire, or from various kinds of plastic mesh. Basically the planting method is much the same for any really good arrangement. Because the base is curved stand the empty frame in the top of a bucket or in a special holder to plant it up rather than let it roll about on the table top.

First line the frame with a good layer of damp sphagnum moss about half an inch thick. This will keep the soil from falling out, will hold moisture well and will allow some of the plants and shoots to grow through it. In the base and under the moss place the saucer mentioned earlier. Now fill the basket with the soil or compost mixture: choose one that is fairly rich and retentive of moisture, possibly one of the soil-less composts.

When planting knock the plants from their pots and so position them that they grow outwards and downwards rather than upwards. Choose a certain amount of trailing material which will cascade down the sides and hide the actual basket. Some small plants can be inserted through the mesh and the moss on the underside of the basket so that they grow downwards and it is even possible to insert a few seeds of something like tropaeolum or nasturtium so that when they germinate they too will grow downwards in festoons of colour. Leave a shallow depression in the soil at the top to facilitate watering.

Water the newly planted basket very thoroughly

and then leave it to drain before it is set in position. Remember that whenever your hanging basket is watered properly it is going to drip, so allow for this if the basket is indoors by placing a bowl in a strategic position for the first half hour. If baskets are hung outdoors where passers-by are likely to be showered some barrier or warning notice should be erected until the drips have finished. Remember that a hanging basket must be growing abundantly to be attractive, although this growth can be of interesting foliage rather than vivid flowers. So feed regularly and probably a little more often than is your normal habit. You may find it helpful to top-dress the baskets with a little fresh soil mixture after they have been on exhibition for a few weeks.

Dead-heading will force the plants to send out more flowers frequently and will keep the baskets looking clean and groomed. On no account let dead plants hang from the baskets and if by some mischance they have been neglected then remove the entire basket and plant it up afresh.

HERBS AND STRAWBERRIES

Another way of using your containers is to grow foods in them. Naturally one would not plant potatoes or cabbages in a container, but certain other subjects are ideal. For example, where there is no garden, how delightful it would be to grow your own fresh herbs in a container on the balcony or roof. There is no reason at all why many of our normal culinary herbs should not be grown quite successfully in containers. Choose your herbs carefully. You may wish to have fresh samples of the common herbs such as mint or parsley, or on the other hand you may prefer to grow the exotics such as tarragon, chervil or dill. If you intend to grow several herbs make quite sure that if they are to share the same container they are compatible. Some like a hot, dry site and well-drained soil while others prefer cooler and moister conditions.

Consider also growing strawberries in a strawberry barrel. This is not difficult, but if you do consider it make sure that you do it well. There are matters of technique which must be mastered to get a good crop. For example, strawberries must get good light and preferably good sunlight. The ordinary strawberry barrel placed out in the full sun will still not get exposure for all its plants unless the barrel is turned to allow the entire circumference to benefit. So mount the barrel on castors or stand it on a platform which can be turned.

Strawberries must also be moist at the roots and this is not always easy to achieve in a barrel. When water is applied to the top it tends to flow out through the upper holes. Whether the barrel is the normal timber, coopered type with 2in holes bored in the sides, or whether it is the terracotta type with purpose-made holes, the method of culture is the same. First make sure that there are drainage holes in the base and above this insert a good layer of drainage material. Use a rich soil mixture and during the growing season feed the plants well in order to get fat and juicy fruits. Begin filling the barrel with the soil mixture until you reach the lowest row of planting holes. Insert the strawberry plants, spreading the roots through the interior soil and firming them in position. Then add more soil until you reach the next layer of planting holes. At this point insert your special watering system. In the centre of the barrel stand a plastic drainpipe so that its base is on the lowest layer of soil, not right through to the layer of drainage material. Fill this drainpipe with small pebbles or clinker as the barrel itself is filled and planted up. When the top of the barrel is reached

Strawberries can be grown in a barrel in holes made over its surface

89

An old strawberry pot filled with twining ivy has an air of ancient charm

the drainpipe can be pulled out and will leave the central core of drainage material in place. Water and liquid fertilisers will now be carried right down through all levels of the soil and so will reach all the plants from top to bottom. Further strawberry plants can be placed on top of the barrel of course.

Make sure that the soil is kept moist at all times and that the sun reaches the entire circumference of the barrel in equal proportions.

# 10

# CARE AND MAINTENANCE

All plants grown in containers live a somewhat artificial life. They live in a soil which has been specially prepared and is richer and more concentrated than ordinary garden soil. They are constantly warmer at the roots than they would be in the garden soil. Their roots are constantly on the point of drying out and then being flushed with moisture once again. Some plants have room and enough and others may have their roots so twisted and confined that their top growth is dwarfed. Other plants are expected to grow under the most artificial conditions, on a roof top or balcony, hanging suspended in the air, cramped in a container ten times too small.

It would be reasonable to expect that container-grown plants might be particularly susceptible to disease or to insect attack because of the artificiality of their lives; yet this is not so. Those plants that are particularly open to visitations from such pests as greenfly and blackfly will probably continue to be so visited, and those plants notoriously susceptible to attacks by viruses, rusts and mildews will probably still have to contend with them, but these problems come with the nature of the plants rather than because of the way they are grown.

Container-grown plants, isolated and separated from the soil, suffer almost none of the soil-borne pests or diseases. No snails or slugs attack them unless eggs have been imported with the soil or unless the gardener has allowed a certain slackness in his grooming.

When the weather is hot and sunny day after day or perhaps when warm winds blow, and the plants require watering perhaps twice a day, there is a danger that this chore will so occupy one that other details of gardening are forgotten. For example one becomes so preoccupied in soaking the soil in a container that one misses entirely the fact that the tender growing shoots at the top of the plant are crawling with aphids or that the blooms are spent and brown and should be removed to give new blossoms a chance.

Both for their health and for their appearance container-grown plants demand a great deal of grooming. It is a comparatively simple matter when working on a garden bed or border to have nearby a wheelbarrow or other receptacle which can receive dead flowers and leaves, weeds and the general debris that is always to be found. But contained plants are fewer in number, quicker to service and frequently in positions on terrace, by steps, in a porch or beside a wall where it is difficult to take a barrow. There is then the problem of what to do with the debris collected. The answer is simply to carry with you a large polythene bag into which everything can be slipped and which can then be emptied in the rubbish bin or on the compost heap at the end of the tour.

Take also what tools might be necessary, including not only a trowel but secateurs or garden scissors, knife, watering-can, raffia or twist ties and even a spare label or two either to replace one which is lost or to mark a plant for some separate and later treatment.

All flowers that have passed their best should be cut away down to the nearest leaf or pair of leaves and then slipped into the plastic bag. Any fallen leaves should be picked up, any new shoots tied in, any weak supports strengthened. Some shoots may be crossing and should be corrected, some may be broken and should be cut back to good wood, some flowers even may be so beautiful that they will be better enjoyed indoors.

Many, perhaps even most, container plants are grown in or near towns, cities or other urban areas. This means almost inevitably that they suffer to some extent from deposits of dirt, dust and perhaps ash or chemicals. This should be cleaned off, particularly from plants with large leaves, such as a fatsia or rhododendron, and particularly again in periods of dry weather, for normally rain does much to clean our plants for us, although admittedly in some areas it falls not so much as rain but as a dilute acid solution! So when watering always include the plant itself if possible rather than the soil alone, and see that all the leaves get a good washing although a gentle one. Some leaves much improve with a light rub from a soft sponge so as to clear accumulations

Annuals give good value. Nasturtiums and dwarf sweet peas will keep this corner of a little courtyard a mass of colour for most of the summer. To promote a long season of bloom it is important that no flowers go to seed. They should be picked off as soon as they fade

of dirt and dust. This is particularly the case with evergreens.

Grooming should take in the containers also. The frequent watering demanded by container plants means that soil and dust are sometimes apt to spatter the sides of containers and if these are white this shows immediately and gives a slovenly look to the entire ensemble. So try to keep containers clean. Keep them also in good repair and well painted where this is necessary. Timber containers or tubs inevitably begin to crack and peel, perhaps even rot in places. Coopered tubs begin to show rust. These may be little points but they all count.

Weeds are seldom a problem of any significance, for normally they are seen at a glance and removed easily. But where a container has been cleared of its faded crop of annuals, for example, or where a single plant in a group has failed and has properly been removed, it is possible that weeds will take over while you are still trying to decide which plants should fill the vacant space or while you are still trying to find the time to carry out the task. Nature not only abhors a vacuum, she usually fills it. So always try to keep containers not only full but overflowing. Remember that you are feeding more heavily and so your plants can still flourish although packed closely together.

Do not attempt to economise on soils or composts. When the soil in a container has grown a certain crop for a year do not expect it to give good service for another. If the container is large and to clear it entirely of soil and drainage material to replace it with fresh will be a considerable task, then remove only the top few inches of soil and replace this with fresh. All used soil can be applied to beds and borders in the garden where it will gradually become refreshed by its contact with the earth. 'Artificial' soils such as the peat-based composts and even vermiculite and the like can be added to garden soil without doing any harm.

Where a container is growing a tree or shrub which has occupied this home for more than a year or two the soil will sometimes tend to pan down and become a solid mass. Undoubtedly the wise thing to do is to replace a part of the soil every year or two, but this is not always possible and is certainly an expensive process. Instead the surface can be teased and scratched to open it up to the air. If a 'mulch' of gravel or chippings is applied to the top of the soil this will serve to some extent to keep the soil open and aerated.

Of course panning of the soil is encouraged by the absolutely vital and necessary watering that the plant receives. This damage can be reduced by spreading gravel on the surface of the soil and it can also be helped by intelligent watering.

Where watering is carried out by means of a watering-can a fine rose should always be used for seedlings and when the plant itself is to be drenched. The rose can be dispensed with when the soil alone is to be moistened. In this case water directly onto the soil and very close to it so that no powerful jet of water is likely to bore a hole into the surface and expose roots. When a hose is used a fine spray can be achieved by means of a special nozzle and this again should be used for watering seedlings and soaking plants. When the soil alone is to be moistened it is best to take off the nozzle and run the water directly onto the soil. If the jet is still too strong, then it can be softened by running it onto the back of a spade or some other tool which will break the main force yet allow the water to soak in quickly.

And finally, if certain of your containers must for various reasons always look their very best the way to do this is to have two or even three identical containers and bring one or two on behind the scenes, as it were, while the first is on public display. When this is past its best it can be taken away and a fresh example can take its place. An alternative is to have separate inner containers which will fit inside the showy outers. The interiors can be of galvanised tin or some substance which is not particularly pleasing to the eye. The separate container plan is particularly helpful for window boxes. These must really be at their very best all the time and this is just not possible, so alternative interiors which can be substituted when necessary keep the exterior of the building always looking bright and attractive.

# 11

# PLANTS FOR CONTAINERS

## TREES AND SHRUBS

One thing we must accept with all trees and shrubs which are to be grown in containers is that they cannot be expected to live in such confined circumstances for ever. After a period of from two to ten years they should be removed from their containers and planted in the open soil where they will undoubtedly show their gratitude by out-performing themselves.

It will be obvious that the major qualifying element in the selection of trees and shrubs will be the size of the container. The larger our containers the wider the list of trees and shrubs that can be accommodated. But this is not the end of the matter, for some trees and shrubs will never live successfully for long periods in a container because of the nature of their roots, the habit of their growth or their sheer size. When you consider that in very general terms the spread of a tree's roots correspond roughly to the spread of its branches above the ground, it will be seen that even if these roots are coiled round and round in the container rather than travelling out more or less straight as they would in the open ground, they will still demand more space than can normally be provided by any container.

The first quality we must look for then in any tree or shrub for container growing is limited growth. For although it is certainly possible to grow a tree from a young seedling up to 10ft or more in height, in time it will begin to suffer, will take on certain dwarf characteristics, will become misshapen and more and more unlike a true, healthy specimen of that type.

One of the major problems of contained plants is the amount of wind they receive in many of their locations. A 10ft tree growing quite happily in a lightweight plastic tub can easily be blown over by a strong gust of wind. A smaller tree may have its foliage seared and burnt by hot winds blowing over a sun-baked patio. Under more normal conditions both these trees would receive considerable protection from neighbouring trees and shrubs.

If any plants, whether they be trees or herbaceous, are so tall, so whippy or so soft in growth that they must be staked, then this presents a real problem to the container gardener, for nothing looks worse than a plant with its corsets showing. There are also very real difficulties in the way of inserting the stake into what is usually quite shallow soil so that it remains rigid and vertical in spite of strong winds. For herba-

96

ceous material it is frequently possible to insert a few bushy twigs before the plants have grown too large and these will give the necessary support yet be hidden as the plants grow through them. For trees and shrubs, if a stake is absolutely necessary then it should be tied in as neatly and inconspicuously as possible and should be dispensed with as soon as the tree is strong enough to look after itself.

Plants in containers are continuously under the spotlight. They do not merge into the background as do other garden plants. So in winter, where a deciduous plant in the border, or indeed even a specimen plant growing in the lawn, will suit the general atmosphere of dormancy, a deciduous tree or shrub in a container will look naked, somehow almost embarrassing.

For these reasons it is always best where possible to choose evergreen plants for the more permanent and year-round residents of containers and this I have very largely done in the following pages. There are plenty of deciduous trees and shrubs that can be used as long as they are removed to a place of decent obscurity during the months when they appear only as skeletons and then brought out again to gain the admiration they deserve when they are bursting into leaf and flower.

Some of the acers or maples, particularly the comparatively dwarf Japanese varieties, make excellent container subjects. They are completely individual with their brilliantly coloured leaves, sometimes finely cut and dissected, and the attractively twisted or bent shape of the main trunk. These Japanese maples do not like a hot sun or a strong wind, so if possible place them where they get shade during the hottest part of the day and where the strongest winds will not sweep directly over them. *Acer palmatum* '*Atropurpureum*' has reddish-purple foliage and a thick and bushy habit. *A. palmatum* '*Dissectum Purpureum*' goes a step further with its finely cut foliage and its bent, gnarled and spreading nature. Very similar is *A. palmatum* '*Dissectum Palmatifidum*', but with bright and vivid green foliage. One of the best cultivars of *A. palmatum* is '*Osakazuki*', particularly brilliant in the autumn.

*Andromeda polifolia*, the marsh rosemary, has several forms, all dwarf and suited to growing in containers and producing almost globular pink flowers in the early summer. It is an evergreen which must have a moist and lime-free soil.

The shrubby *Artemisia abrotanum* which grows 3–4ft high is popularly known as southernwood or lad's love. Like some of its herbaceous relatives it is a culinary herb with aromatic foliage. The flowers it produces are comparatively insignificant, but the evergreen, silvery-grey, lacy, fern-like foliage is its main attraction. It is best cut almost down to soil level each spring and allowed to produce young, clean, fresh foliage again.

It is also the foliage of the aucuba which commends it, although if there are two or more bushes of different sexes the females will produce their attractive and glossy red berries. There are a number of forms of *Aucuba japonica*, some with attractively mottled and splashed leaves, gold and green, some with white or yellow berries, some large and some small. They make good, tough, evergreen shrubs for containers, thriving in sun or shade and under the conditions of polluted air found in so many cities.

There are too many azaleas for them to be listed here but the Japanese varieties in particular are suitable for container culture. Evergreen and brilliantly flowered, these little shrubs are most highly commended, with their wide range of flower colour in late spring and early summer and good

value from the foliage at other times. Consult a good catalogue or go to a garden centre at the right time of year and choose colours that particularly appeal to you or will blend with the surroundings. Remember that azaleas must have a moist and peaty soil and protection from the sun when it is at its hottest. Do not plant too deeply, but get the top of the root ball a fraction below the rim of the container where it is just covered by the peaty soil.

There are a number of varieties of berberis that make splendid container plants and with their coloured foliage and their splendid flowers and fruits they can be quite magnificent. But they have one fault which to me removes them from our lists immediately, and that is their spiteful, thorny spines. I have said earlier that container plants need constant grooming and this task is highly unpleasant to carry out with the berberis. But if you are horny-handed try some of them. Many are evergreen, all are colourful.

Entirely different is the pleasant little box, gentle, small-leaved and almost asking to be handled and clipped into various formal shapes. It is an easy evergreen. *Buxus sempervirens* is the common box and a somewhat more interesting variety is *B. elegantissima*, with a grey and cream foliage which gives the bush a silver appearance. Box will grow in sun or shade.

The camellia is one of the best-known plants for growing in tubs and other containers and small wonder, for given just a little protection from the worst of the north and east winds they will grace the site at all times with their handsome, glossy evergreen foliage and produce gorgeous flowers. There are many camellias from which to choose, with flowers coloured from white through pink to the deepest red. They like a lime-free soil which should be kept moist at all times.

A tiny area is made to look more spacious if it is paved and furnished with potted plants. Here, stone textures and walls have been used attractively to foster the illusion of space but at the same time they give protection to the plants. Upright shrubs, trailing, ivy-leaved pelargoniums, agave and heliotrope are used effectively

99

This blue-flowered shrub, *Ceanothus thyrsiflorus repens*, is especially useful against walls

There are so few shrubs with blue flowers that one must grasp at any that are suitable for growing in a pot or tub. Such a one is *Ceanothus thyrsiflorus repens*, an evergreen of low and spreading habit and covered in light blue flowers in May. This variety has proved remarkably hardy, but it produces better flowers if it is given a little shelter in the coldest months. Because of its habit of growth it is excellent against a wall, where it will spread conveniently under a ground-floor window.

More blue is provided by *Ceratostigma willmottianum*, a little shrub which produces its flowers later in the summer and follows them with attractive reddish-brown seed heads. In cold districts the ceratostigma may be cut down by the frosts, but if it is pruned almost to soil level at the beginning of spring it will come up freshly again. This is obviously a deciduous shrub.

Coming from Mexico and so unsuited to northern regions of the English-speaking world, *Choisya ternata* is known otherwise as a hardy evergreen flowering shrub which grows to about 5ft and produces its fragrant, starry white flowers in May. If there is an opportunity of removing the contained plants to a place of shelter (though not necessarily actual warmth) during the winter there is more likelihood of better results later.

Known popularly as the wire-netting bush because of the peculiar angular shapes of its joints, the *Corokia cotoneaster* is an evergreen (though some say deciduous) flowering shrub, tender enough to warrant giving it what wall protection is available. It has little leaves and tiny, starry yellow flowers which are succeeded by orange-red berries. It grows to about 6ft, has no particular preferences for soil, will tolerate a certain amount of wind but likes a sheltered position.

G

The various species and varieties of cotoneaster have proved themselves in many countries to be excellent garden subjects, easy to grow, pleasant in appearance, both flowering and berrying, and attractive to bees. Some of the cotoneasters are equally useful as container plants and there are so many that it would be difficult to choose only one or two for mention. Nearly all have white flowers followed by scarlet berries. They can be trees, shrubs or spreading and prostrate plants. They make no particular demands as to soil, sun, shade or wind. Most are evergreen. Some can be trained upwards as specimens, others will grow against a wall like a climber and still others will grow outwards and downwards over their container sides to cover the ground and conceal a drain cover or some other eyesore. Most useful, even for so difficult a subject as bonsai.

The daphne is a very rewarding shrub for a container. It is small, neat, well covered, easy to grow, floriferous, perfumed and most species are evergreen. In the main the flowers are produced in April, May or June, but earlier bloom, even in January, can be obtained on *D. mezereum*, a deciduous species, and in February from the delicious *D. odora* '*Aureomarginata*'. Once again there is a very wide choice and it is wisest, perhaps, to see plants actually in bloom.

A single specimen tree growing on a single trunk in a container large enough to suit its considerable root spread can seem somewhat naked with the bare soil at its foot. This can be filled with bulbs in the spring and with other dwarf or spreading plants at other times of the year, but one of the best 'skirts' is heath, or erica. *Erica carnea* gives splendid winter colour which brings interest to the container. As is so often the case there are many from which to choose and unlike most ericas the carnea range tolerates a certain amount of lime in the soil. In

*Fatsia japonica*, a dramatic plant with glossy green leaves

addition to the flower colour many varieties have vivid foliage tints, mainly gold and orange, which make them as splendid and vivid as any flowering plant.

The usual garden species of euonymus, many known as spindles, are deciduous, and splendid though these may be there are two particular ever-green species which are happily tailored to the requirements of the container. They are *E. fortunei* and *E. japonica*, both of which are blessed with long lists of varieties, usually with differing colour, shape or size of leaf. They will grow in almost any soil, in sun or in shade, they are hardy and as their main attraction is their foliage they do not suffer by seasonal differences.

A dramatic plant with great foot-wide, palmate, glossy green leaves is the *Fatsia japonica*. It will grow quite large, thick and heavy. Its flowers and the berries which follow are visually subordinate to the magnificent foliage. It likes a little shade but is tolerant of most other conditions.

The American wych-hazel, *Fothergilla monticola*, is not always easy to grow and it is deciduous, but if there is space and if you have a spare container it is well worth trying for the glory of its brilliant autumn foliage. It is said to be hardy. The fluffy spikes of creamy-white flowers appear in early spring. The fothergilla likes a light, peaty-sandy soil and some shelter from early morning sun and the coldest of the local winds.

Most species of fuchsia come from central and south America and in more northern climates must be grown with the benefit of some protection. A few are hardy, but even these are normally cut to the ground in cold winters so it is questionable whether it is worth growing them in the special conditions applying to containers. But so tender, so beautiful and so romantic are the many kinds, colours and cultivars of fuchsia that it is well worth growing some specimens to grace your containers during the summer. There is a tremendous choice and the best way of selecting plants for your own containers is to go to a specialist nursery and see them growing for yourself. You will in any case get great pleasure from your visit, for there is no such thing as a fuchsia grower who is not happily crazed and besotted with the beauty of his plants and sufficiently enthusiastic to be able to pass on a measure of his delight.

*Helianthemum nummularium*, the well-known sun rose, is an evergreen thick with flowers between mid-May and the end of June. There are many cultivars with flowers of white, cream, yellow, through many pinks to several reds. The plant is neat and low growing, likes a position in the sun and is undemanding in many ways. Unfortunately the helianthemum is so prodigal with its favours that it seems to burn itself out and as a general rule does not live long. It is easily propagated, however, so this is a fault of minor importance.

It is true that hydrangeas can make wonderful plants and that they do well in containers, so to justify my own lack of enthusiasm about them perhaps I should say that they are deciduous, that they need staking if they are grown well and that when they are not actually in flower they are of little interest. They are also plants with a highly dramatic thirst as the name appears to suggest although it actually applies to the shape of the seed vessel, which the Greeks thought was like a water vessel.

A good evergreen with a dual purpose is the sweet bay, *Laurus nobilis*, which of course is the plant from which we get our kitchen bay leaves. It is not a highly decorative tree in itself, but it takes pruning well so that it can be trained into certain formal

Two round-bellied terracotta pots filled with pelargoniums, both attractive and useful

shapes to give it architectural value in the garden. It also stands shade well.

If you are fortunate enough to live in a comparatively mild district you will be able to grow in your containers the New Zealand daisy bush, *Olearia haastii*, an evergreen with silvery leaves and a mass of small, white, daisy-like flowers so thick that they cover the entire bush—one reason why the plant is also called the Victoria snow bush. This is a good plant for the seaside, which means that it stands up to winds. It likes a light soil and does not object to chalk. It should be clipped over each spring to encourage the flowers which appear in midsummer.

Some of the most vivid, dramatic and excitingly beautiful of all plants suited to containers are the pieris, hardy evergreens some of which not only produce whole racemes of dainty white flowers like the lily-of-the-valley but also reveal their new young shoots in the spring as a brilliant and shining red. *Pieris forrestii* and *P. taiwanensis* are two good species, but there are more, as well as several cultivars. Plants like a well-drained but moist and peaty soil and they should be placed in light shade with protection from strong winds. A little winter care, even placing them in a cold greenhouse for the worst of the winter in cold districts, will be amply repaid in the spring.

When we come to the rhododendron family we reach riches indeed, with a real wealth of material from which to choose and with flowers of every colour. If you have space and sufficient containers you can have rhododendrons in flower from February, sometimes even earlier, until about June. There are tremendous numbers of hybrids from which to choose and it is worth while selecting carefully, seeking not only the timing and colour of the flowers you want but also the shape and habit of

growth of the bush. As a general rule the smaller hybrids are better for growing in containers. All rhododendrons must, of course, have a lime-free soil and their roots should not be planted too deeply. This means that specimens in a draughty spot can get blown right out of their containers, so give them some shelter from strong winds. Keep the roots mulched and cool and never allow them to become dry. When plants have finished flowering always remove the little cluster of seed heads which remains. A simple twist is all that is necessary.

Many roses will grow quite happily in a container for some years and it will be obvious that the choice here is too wide to make any recommendations except to say that modern varieties should be grown rather than any of the species of old-fashioned roses, both because of the problem of size and because the modern rose, particularly the floribunda, with its perpetual blooming habit can give us flowers sometimes for as much as five or six months of the year.

Once again we find a lovely plant for containers among the culinary herbs, this time in rue, *Ruta graveolens* 'Jackman's Blue', a small, bushy shrub with wonderful pearly grey-blue foliage. This foliage is the important part of the plant and the yellow flowers which begin to appear in June should be removed before they open. Trim back the entire plant in the spring to keep a good overall shape and appearance.

Curiously similar in some respects is the santolina, again evergreen, or rather ever-silvery-white, with aromatic foliage and yellow flowers. The best form for container growing is probably *Santolina chamaecyparis* 'Nana', dwarf, thick and producing a mass of its yellow flowers in July. Trim the bush back almost to the previous year's growth each spring to produce fresh, attractive foliage and to keep a good shape. It

Probably the best container plant in any temperature or any
climate is the familiar pelargonium or pot geranium

will grow well in the sun. Remove all flowers as they fade in order to get a constant succession.

There are a tremendous number of conifers which could be listed, but their sheer number, their close similarity and the complexity of some of their names suggest that it will probably be better for readers to choose by looking at them in a garden centre rather than from a list. They make excellent container plants and are particularly useful for their architectural value in the garden. They need not be green only, for silver, glaucous blue and gold are among the colours available and the gold in particular can be as bright as any flower colour during the dark days of winter. Some are very quick-growing so these should be excluded from your lists. Others are either dwarf in habit or so slow-growing that they can occupy a container for twenty years without outgrowing it.

## HERBACEOUS PLANTS

Almost every herbaceous plant will grow in a container, so in order to keep this book to manageable proportions it is necessary to reject some. Some plants are so tall or so floppy that they require disciplined staking, and we have (I hope) agreed that stakes are hideous in containers. There are also a number of plants which, although they do not necessarily always need staking, are so tall that they would look quite out of proportion growing in a container—as an example think merely of some of the delphiniums. Some herbaceous plants must be rejected because their life is too short. It is certainly possible to use containers to display a constantly changing series of little flowering plants and this may well be a charming thing to do, but for most of us it simply is not practical. We cannot spare the time. For this reason plants listed here have a comparatively long life, although this does not mean that

they will be in bloom most of the season but rather that in bloom or not they will bring something of interest to the scene.

Personally I feel that the best advice I can give in choosing herbaceous plants for containers is to be adventurous and experimental. If you try to grow a certain plant and for some reason you fail, then there is very little lost. On the other hand you could very well find that confined roots and constant attention will transform an unlikely container plant into a favourite.

I do not list plants as annuals, biennials or perennials but simply as herbaceous. It will also be noted that without going into specific detail only the genus of the plants is given. This does not mean that all species and all varieties are suitable, but that in the genus one or more can successfully be grown in containers. The lists do not pretend to be complete nor are they intended to be more than a rough guide of what can sometimes be grown in containers given certain advantages such as a helpful climate and either a lack of wind or a sheltered spot. It is not suggested that all the plants listed can be grown anywhere. The important thing, as I have said, is to experiment. Many of these plants can be grown from seed, others can be bought in markets, from street stalls, in florists' shops and at garden centres as young plants ready for planting in your containers. Make sure all danger of frost is past before you attempt this, unless of course the plant is quite hardy.

*Acanthus*  Large, glossy green leaves of architectural value and spikes of lavender flowers in summer. Cut flower spikes almost to soil level after flowering.

*Achillea*  Dwarf species are best for containers.

*Aconitum*

*Adonis*

*Aethionema*   Flowers, usually rose pink, will cover the soil.

*Agapanthus*   Choose hybrids of hardy species.

*Agave*   Long lived, but only try them in frost-free places.

*Ageratum*

*Ajuga*   Good ground cover.

*Alchemilla*   Useful, easy, self-sowing.

*Allium*   Hardy decorative onions with astonishingly beautiful flower heads which will dry well.

*Alstroemeria*   Dead-head regularly for flower succession.

*Alyssum*   Familiar, but still good for carpeting, for dry-stone walls and the like.

*Amaryllis*   Gorgeous flowers from this bulb, but give it shelter in cold areas.

*Anagallis*   Red or blue pimpernel. Give them full sun.

*Anchusa*

*Anthemis*   Some excellent hybrids among these chamomiles.

*Antirrhinum*

*Arabis*   Keep them in containers for they can be invasive in the open garden.

*Armeria*   Long-lasting little flowers.

*Artemisia*   Both herbaceous and shrubby species do well.

*Asclepias*   The smaller species are probably the best for containers.

*Asperula*   Several, all good.

*Aster*   Many of the michaelmas daisies do well.

*Astilbe*   The dwarfer hybrids are probably best, but all look well associated with water.

*Astrantia*   Will take sun or shade.

*Aubrietia*

Balm (*Melissa*)   A useful herb. Choose the golden variety.

*Baptisia*   May need twiggy support if too tall.

*Begonia*   Tremendous choice of types and colours.

*Bellis*   The common daisy and its varieties still take some beating.

*Bergenia*   Evergreen with fine, large leaves turning vivid red tones in autumn.

*Calceolaria*   There are hardy, alpine species.

*Calendula*   Many marigold varieties are useful.

*Callirhoe*   Some of the perennial species, from the southern United States, do well in sun and will stand drought.

*Callistephus*   Do not grow these china asters in the same container in consecutive years because of wilt.

*Campanula*   A wide choice here.

*Centaurea*   There are good, hardy, compact varieties.

*Cheiranthus*   Dwarf wallflowers may have a short life but they bring rich colour to it.

*Chelone*   Pretty pink flowers but may need supporting with twigs.

*Chionodoxa*   Charming hardy bulbs.

*Chrysanthemum*   Many opportunities here.

*Cineraria*   Really better indoors. Bright and colourful but subject to too many pests and diseases.

Clary (*Salvia sclarea*)   Full sun for this culinary herb.

*Colchicum*   Attractive flowering bulbs.

*Coleus*   Foliage more vivid than many flowers.

*Coreopsis*   Of the perennial species there are some first-class American varieties.

*Crocus*

*Cyclamen*   Some of the hardy species are delightful as underplantings to taller trees or shrubs.

*Dianthus*   Many of the pinks and sweet williams do well if given plenty of sun and a well-drained soil mixture.

*Dicentra*   Graceful and elegant plants, best given some shelter from strong winds.

All varieties of chrysanthemums, like this pompon 'Bronze Fairie', are suitable for containers

*Dictamnus*  Much better than the better-known Kochia with which it is sometimes confused. This is a perennial not an annual.

*Doronicum*  Can be in flower almost from early spring to late autumn if dead-headed carefully.

*Erigeron*  Go for the longer-lived, larger, brighter varieties rather than the species. For the sun.

*Erodium*  Excellent on or beside a limestone wall.

*Eschscholzia*  Many varieties of the popular Californian poppy.

*Euphorbia*  Look among the perennial species for good, solid, 'background' container colour.

*Exacum*  A bushy evergreen with purple flowers for about three months of the year.

*Gaillardia*  Many good hybrids available.

*Gazania*  A similar and related daisy.

*Geranium*  The crane's-bills, not to be confused with the pelargoniums, are among the most useful plants in the garden and many are excellent for containers.

*Geum*  Long-lasting flowers of yellow, orange, scarlet.

*Gilia*  Tall or short, all do well in sun.

*Godetia*  Vivid single or double flowers.

*Helenium*  Still another free-flowering daisy.

*Heliopsis*  Single and double varieties, usually with orange, lemon, gold or yellow flowers.

*Hemerocallis*  There are a number of good day lily hybrids.

*Heuchera*  There are some good, well-coloured hybrids.

*Hosta*  Although grown mainly for their foliage the hostas also provide us with attractive flowers. Grow in shade.

*Hypericum*  There are many and most are valuable for they give flowers followed by berries and brilliantly-coloured foliage. Place in the sun.

*Iberis*  Some of the hardy evergreen perennial varieties are the best choice for containers.

*Impatiens*  There are some splendid new hybrids.

*Incarvillea*  Long-lasting pinkish flowers.

*Kochia*  Use as an effective architectural plant.

*Lamium*  Some of the dead-nettles can be useful as a ground cover under a specimen tree or shrub.

*Lewisia*  Some good hybrids, but never allow them to get or stay wet in the winter or you will lose them.

*Limnanthes*  The 'poached egg flower' is attractive to bees.

*Linaria*  Many varieties available.

*Lychnis*  Flowers from white through pink and orange to red.

*Lysimachia*  A useful and attractive trailer, but invasive if it gets into the open ground.

*Lythrum*  There are good new varieties here.

*Matthiola*  There are many good stocks for containers.

*Mertensia*  Bell-shaped blue flowers.

*Mesembryanthemum*  A vivid creeping succulent for full sun.

*Molucella*  Bells of Ireland is only half hardy but 'all-green' flowers are popular. These can be dried.

*Monarda*  Many good varieties, all liked by butterflies and bees.

*Nemesia*  Many colourful hybrids.

*Nepeta*  Really a ground-cover plant.

*Nicotiana*  Worth growing for the scent alone.

*Oenothera*  A wide and useful range available here.

*Omphalodes*  Like a larger forget-me-not.

*Oxalis*  Can become a garden weed if allowed to roam.

*Papaver*  For sheer colour we cannot ignore the poppies.

*Pelargonium*  Perhaps the best known and most used of all container plants, and with good reason.

*Penstemon*   Wide range of colours available.

*Petunia*   Vivid and multi-coloured, large or smaller flowered, tall or dwarf, upright or pendulous.

*Phlox*   There is a wide and useful range.

*Physostegia*   Snapdragon-like flowers, mainly white or pink.

*Polygonatum*   The lovely Solomon's seal has also some good relatives.

*Polygonum*   There are some useful herbaceous species.

*Potentilla*   The garden hybrids are probably best for containers.

*Primula*   Several different useful kinds.

*Pulsatilla*   Like anemones, several colours.

*Pyrethrum*   Popular daisies.

*Ranunculus*   Some good buttercups here.

*Reseda*   It is almost essential to have a tub or trough of sweet scented mignonette.

*Rodgersia*   Good foliage as well as flowers, but keep out of strong winds and bright sun.

*Rudbeckia*   Still another useful golden daisy.

*Sanvitalia*   Prostrate, creeping, yellow flowers.

*Saponaria*   The hardy perennial with double white or pink flowers is best.

*Saxifraga*   Many kinds, many colours.

*Scabiosa*   Many colours available in the varieties.

*Sedum*   Several good stonecrops can be chosen.

*Sempervivum*   The houseleeks give further choice.

*Smilacina*   Keep cool, moist and shaded.

*Solidago*   Choose from some of the smaller garden hybrids.

*Stachys*   Some good hybrids are available.

*Stokesia*   In flower for several months.

*Tagetes*   There are many excellent varieties among these African marigolds.

*Thymus*   Mainly creeping or mat-forming, but available in vivid colours.

*Tiarella*   Forms neat clumps of mainly white flowers.

*Verbascum*   Do not try the tall species in containers for they will need staking. There are plenty of lower-growing varieties.

*Verbena*   Worth growing for their scent.

*Veronica*   Many useful varieties available.

*Vinca*   Periwinkle.

*Viola*   Many kinds.

*Zantedeschia*   Various forms of arum lilies, frequently seen in containers in Mediterranean countries.

*Zinnia*   A wide range of colours.

## TREES AND SHRUBS SUITABLE FOR BONSAI

*Acer, Azalea, Betula, Carpinus, Chamaecyparis, Cotoneaster, Crataegus, Cryptermeria, Fagus, Forsythia, Ginkgo, Juniperus, Larix, Malus, Picea, Pinus, Prunus, Quercus, Thuja, Ulmus.*

## PLANTS SUITABLE FOR MINIATURE OR SINK GARDENS

**Perrenials.** *Androsace, Arabis, Armeria, Asperula, Campanula, Dianthus, Draba, Erinus, Erodium, Gentiana, Geranium, Polygala, Raoulia, Saxifraga, Sedum, Sempervivum, Silene, Soldanella, Veronica, Viola.*

**Trees and Shrubs.** *Cassiope, Chamaecyparis, Genista, Helianthemum, Jasminum, Juniperus, Micromeria, Pieris, Polygala, Rhododendron, Spirea, Veronica.*

## PLANTS FOR A HERB GARDEN

Angelica, balm (*Melissa officinalis*), basil (*Ocimum basilicum*), borage, caraway (*Carum carvi*), chervil (*Anthriscus cerefolium*), chives (*Allium schoenoprasum*), clary (*Salvia sclarea*), dill (*Peucedanum graveolens*), fennel, garlic (*Allium sativum*), hyssop, lavender, lovage (*Ligusticum scoticum*), marjoram (*Origanum*), mint (*Mentha*), parsley (*Carum petroselinum*), rosemary, rue (*Ruta graveolens*), sage (*Salvia officinalis*), salad burnet (*Sanguisorba minor*), savory (*Satureja*), sorrel (*Rumex*), sweet bay (*Laurus nobilis*), tarragon (*Artemisia dracunculus*), thyme.

## PLANTS FOR A BOTTLE GARDEN

Suitable plants will depend on the size of the container. Choose slow growers and no plants which flower. Some, but by no means all, members of the following families will be suitable, but to get them you may have to place a special order with a nurseryman or grow your own small plants from seed or cuttings.

*Begonia rex, Croton, Cryptanthus, Cyperus, Ficus pumila* and *F. radicans, Fittonia argyroneura* and *F. verschaffeltii, Hedera* (small-leaf varieties), *Helxine soleirolii, Maranta leuconeura kerchoveana* and *M. makoyana, Pellionia pulchra,* *Peperomia caperata, Saxifraga sarmentosa, Sellaginella, Sonerila.*

## PLANTS FOR HANGING BASKETS

It is impossible to be dogmatic about plants for hanging baskets, for the choice will depend on the size of the basket, whether it will be in sun or shade, whether foliage or flowering plants are preferred, annuals or perennials, and finally, of course, on the taste and preferences of the gardener. Many plants will succeed so long as they are kept moist at the roots and there is no reason why there should be a mixture rather than a basket filled entirely with one kind of plant. The following list is of perennials which are known to be successful:

*Achimenes, Ageratum, Begonia, Columnea, Fuchsia, Hoya, Lachenalia, Plectranthus, Saxifraga, Tradescantia, Zebrina* and *Zygocactus.*

# INDEX

*Figures in italic denote illustrations*